*From*

*Freedom*

*to*

*Slavery*

*Gerry
Spence*

ST. MARTIN'S GRIFFIN

*From*

# FREEDOM

*to*

# SLAVERY

*The
Rebirth
of
Tyranny
in
America*

NEW YORK

*For John C. Johnson*

*my dear friend,*

*who joyously proves every day*

*that freedom can be achieved*

*by embracing both life and death*

*as partners in the cosmos.*

*Design by Jaye Zimet*
*Photographs by Gerry Spence*

*ISBN 0-312-14342-7*

*10   9   8   7   6   5   4   3   2*

# C O N T E N T S

CONTENTS

# About the Trial of Randy Weaver

*The story of Randy Weaver's trial was not contained in the* original edition of this book, for I had delivered the manuscript to the publisher some months before the trial had begun. Hence Chapter 1 of *From Freedom to Slavery* contains only that portion of the story as I knew it *before* the trial. In this edition, and for the first time, I recount the egregious revelations of the trial itself as well as some of the damning conclusions of the Justice Department's investigation of the federal officers who engaged in this infamous war on our citizens. I will show how the United States Attorney and his assistant were responsible for the erroneous charges that were brought against Weaver in the first place. This story is recounted as Chapter 2, and has not been heretofore published anywhere.

I tried the Weaver case with the assistance of three very able, loyal and dedicated lawyers, Chuck Peterson, Gary Gilman and my son, Kent, without whose continuous support and wise advice the acquittal of Randy Weaver could not have been accomplished. Jeannie Bontadelli, my assistant, worked tirelessly in tracking our cross-examination through thousands of pages of testimony and witness statements, as often accompany a case of this length and magnitude. Gary Gilman of Boise and my team from Jackson contributed our labor and our expenses to the defense of Randy Weaver, for there are, indeed, cases of such principle and such enormity that a trial lawyer, if he be a true trial lawyer, must rise to the call whether he be paid for his services or not. Indeed, there are cases, as this, that are of such proportion that it becomes a deep and rare privilege for any attorney to there ply his noble art.

When I took the case, Chuck Peterson of Boise, hearing of my involvement, volunteered his services, got himself appointed by the court to represent Randy, and received only the usual shamefully penurious stipend provided by the government to appointed defense counsel, a token payment that would guarantee the bankruptcy of many skilled lawyers in private practice. David Nevin and Ellison Matthews, who obtained Kevin Harris's acquittal based on the law of self-defense, received the same inadequate stipend but nevertheless proved themselves not only as greatly gifted trial lawyers but as our loyal friends and colleagues as well.

I have not attempted to include the various arguments of the government attorneys. Those arguments were, in most part, rejected by the jury. This account, therefore, is solely from the perspective of the defense, which, itself, is in accordance with the rule of law that provides that all evidence offered to the jury by the side who prevails in the case, as well as all reasonable inferences arising therefrom, will be taken as true.

The shocking, dastardly explosion at Oklahoma City in April of 1995 has once more thrust the scandalous story of the Randy Weaver case to the national forefront, along with a profusion of political and philosophical questions. The fact that Weaver's name continues to be mentioned in light of Oklahoma City suggests that he still is associated, erroneously, with far-right violence and that his acquittal of all major charges at the trial has never afforded him the vindication that a man might expect to enjoy who has been found "not guilty" by a jury of his peers. Instead, Randy Weaver has been viciously tarred and feathered by the government and the media, both in and out of the courtroom. People seem to remember the bad things the longest. They remember the accusations that he was a black-arm-banded skinhead, who was associated with wrong-headed punks. People remember that a federal marshal was killed in a shoot-out, and that Weaver was accused of having killed the marshal. Understandably, people don't have much tolerance for such carryings-on.

I remember once having defended Ed Cantrell, the last of the old fast-draw gunfighters, the top lawman in the small western town of Rock Springs, Wyoming. Cantrell had shot an undercover agent, Michael Rosa, neatly between the eyes on the eve Rosa was expected to testify against Cantrell before a statewide grand jury. Cantrell shot Rosa in front of a couple of other cops, but the defense, as in all gunfight cases, was self-defense, and when the jury acquitted Cantrell, well, the press raised hell. It was a stinking miscarriage of justice accomplished by a smooth-talking lawyer, namely your friend, Gerry Spence.

After Cantrell was acquitted, I commiserated with Cantrell about how people wouldn't accept the jury's verdict, and how they'd rather believe what they'd read in the papers or seen on *Sixty Minutes* instead of the evidence the jury heard under oath in the courtroom. After a long silence, as was often the way of conversations with Cantrell, he said in that voice, deep and almighty sounding as Moses himself, "Fuck 'em, I'm free."

And I remember the indelible defamation laid upon a woman named Imelda Marcos by the one-eyed media, their focus more on what made good reading than what revealed the truth. The vilification of the woman was ubiquitous and unrelenting, this "sow" who dared accumulate three thousand pairs of shoes and who went on wild and decadent shopping sprees with money she had stolen from the starving multitudes of the Philippines. It all made good reading. But it also irreversibly destroyed her public image in America and in many other countries around the world. Out of the thousands of reporters who penned stories about Mrs. Marcos, not one had bothered to ask her where she got all of those shoes. When I asked her myself, she seemed glad to explain. "You see," she said, "the Philippine Islands are one of the world's largest producers of shoes. We have thousands of tiny manufacturers in our country, and every one of them wanted to say that their first lady wore *their* shoes. So they sent their shoes to me, and I put them in the closet. Most of them didn't fit. But I kept them anyway."

Day after day during her long trial, I encountered the venomous stories in the press about how the government's witnesses were nailing the guilty Mrs. Marcos to the cross. With only small word changes, the stories all came out the same. The media's accounts of the trial embellished the tainted testimony of the prosecution witnesses who, themselves, feared retaliation by the Aquino government in the Philippines should the witnesses choose not to testify for the government. I cross-examined something like ninety witnesses in the case, and not one of them laid a glove on the woman. I never called a witness in her defense. Nor did I call Mrs. Marcos to the stand. I didn't need to. And the jury acquitted her—that's how weak the government's honest case was against this woman.

Yet I remember a malevolently unflattering picture of Mrs. Marcos that took up the entire front page of one of the New York tabloids. Under the picture, in four-inch-high headlines, screamed the single word, "Oink!". When at a traffic light, I saw a newsboy approaching our van holding up the paper, I tried to divert Mrs. Marcos' attention, but she saw it. I could see the flash of hurt cloud her eyes.

"I'm sorry," I said.

"That's all right," she replied. "That's not me." And it wasn't. And it never had been. Yet today she is as hated in America as ever, the truth and the jury's verdict notwithstanding.

In the Randy Weaver case, the same pernicious dynamic has been in operation now for some time. Once smeared with the stink of guilt, the accused can rarely be cleansed, not even by a jury's verdict. According to those in the media who purport to know, Randy Weaver, too, was guilty. He just had good lawyers who got him off. Many had remembered, slightly, this slight man. Some called him a white supremacist, some a separatist. Some called him a racist and a Nazi. Many hated him. A few who had followed the case remembered he had been brought to trial for the murder of Marshal William Degan, and to answer a kitchen sink full of other charges, such as a conspiracy with his family to create a violent confrontation with law enforcement officials, sawing off some shotguns, failing to appear at trial to answer the charge of sawing off the shotguns, assaulting federal marshals, shooting at a helicopter, possessing firearms while a fugitive from justice, committing the above crimes while he was on probation and, if that weren't enough, carrying firearms during the commission of a violent crime.

After the trial in 1993, a few of Randy's sympathizers wrote me letters and said kind things, like "You will be repaid in heaven for your work," and I wrote them back and told them I was grateful for their letters. A few sent me checks for five dollars and fifty dollars, and I sent the checks on to Randy. He needed them worse than I, for Randy was unemployed, had the motherless child, Elisheba, at home to care for, and the family was destitute. Later, a few folks stood in the lines at my book signings to say simple things like, "Thank you for what you did for Randy Weaver," and I sat there at the tables in the bookstores writing their names into the front of their books and signing my own name, with best wishes to them. At times, I looked up into their serious faces, and I saw their eyes, and I thought of the faces of the neighbors of my boyhood in Wyoming, and of the hard times and the hard frames of working men in freshly pressed bib overalls who mowed their lawns a week late in August and who went to church on Christmas and Easter, and who, on the other Sundays of the year, went fishing at Lake DeSmit in their old rowboats, or, in the winter, who fished through the ice for rainbow trout. In the fall you could find these same old boys camped up on Spring Creek or Bull Creek in the Big Horns, hunters like my father, with their ancient 30–40 Krags and their 30–aught–6 Springfields, and their 45–70's with the heavy octagonal barrels, big game guns that were right for elk, and if a buck deer came bounding through the timber, right for him too.

And now, years later, these same sort of folks came out to my book signing, people with open, unmade faces and quick, generous smiles, and as they told me how they appreciated my having defended Randy Weaver, they would reach out for my hand to shake it before they asked me to sign their books, like shaking my hand was that important. By these spontaneous remembrances I had always felt well paid for my defense of the man who, had he a whit, would surely have paid me himself.

But after the Oklahoma horror, after the broken bodies of the dead babies were held up for the people to see and the tired brave men dug for many days against the rubble and the scree mining for the dead, and after the weeping and the crippled and the white-sheeted corpses on the gurneys were pushed up before us on the screens day after day, and we joined in the shock and the sorrow, the media persons, most of whom had given little thought to the meaning of the Weaver case, began to ask their standard questions, often skimmed from the surface of their minds.

Some pretty-faced anchorman, pointing to me in a television interview, would exclaim with his usual concocted excitement: "And here is the man who represented Randy Weaver, the white supremacist who killed a federal marshal!" Then, as anchormen are trained, he would suddenly turn to me, as if to attack. And his first question, as often a statement, would be born on facile, mechanical lips, but with words wrapped in the sound of the unassailable authority of television.

"And, of course, you got him off," the anchorman would add accusingly, as if he had exposed me. And it was then that often I would reach over and gently touch the anchorman on the top of his hand, and say, "Look at me." And when, surprised, he looked at me, I would say, "Randy Weaver didn't kill anyone. He never even fired his gun at anyone. He was charged with murder by the federal government, and they threw in a lot of other crimes to boot, but he was innocent and the jury found him innocent, and the government knew he was innocent all along." And when the anchorman would look away, I would touch his hand again and say again, "Look at me." And when he turned back—even anchormen become obedient on television—I would speak into his eyes quietly, and sometimes I would signal the camera to come up close to watch, and I would ask, "So why have you told the folks that Randy Weaver killed a marshal?"

After that there were rejoinders like, "Well, I thought he killed a marshal," or sometimes the anchorman would ask, "Well, then, what happened?" and I knew he really didn't want to know what happened, but I usually told him the story anyway.

When I would begin by telling how the marshals waited in ambush in their camouflage combat suits with even their faces covered in frightening masks and how the lead marshal, with his machine gun, had shot this small boy's dog in the back—the anchorman would look away again, and then sometimes I would grab the anchorman's wrist lightly, and ask him, "Have you ever seen a dog with its back broken? Have you ever seen a dog yelp and whine so piteously and drag its paralyzed hind legs behind it as it tries to run home?" And sometimes the anchorman would shake his head ever so slightly, no, and sometimes he would try to quickly change the subject. But mostly the anchorman wouldn't say anything, and before they interrupted, as is their habit, I would continue, "And then this little boy shot in the direction of these men who

killed his dog and who were hiding behind cover, behind rocks and trees and stumps in their camouflage
suits, these men, armed to the teeth and waiting at the
ready, their machine guns pointed at this child with a
choirboy's pretty soprano voice. Do you want to know
his name?" And most would nod. What else could they
do? "Sammy was the boy's name. He was barely fourteen years old, but not much larger than a ten-year-
old. And do you want to know what his daddy, Randy
Weaver, who was way up the road, hollered to him?"
And most would nod again. "He hollered, 'Come on
home, Sammy. Come on home, Son.' " Then I would
let silence approach the edge of oppressive, which, on
television, is but the minor part of a second, and just
before the anchorman was about to ask his next question, I would ask mine: "Do you also want to know what
the boy's last words were as he was running home and
just before they opened fire on the boy with their machine guns?" And when they still didn't answer I would
say, "The last words Randy Weaver heard from the lips
of his child were, 'I'm coming Dad.' Then, as Sammy
ran, they opened fire. First they shot his arm nearly
off. Then they shot him in the back, this child without
a single adult hair on his skinny white body, and they
watched him fall in a little heap, and after that they
pretended they didn't know they had killed him. But
Randy Weaver wasn't there when Marshal Degan was
shot. Randy Weaver never shot a person in his life and
never aimed a gun at anyone in his life. That's why I
couldn't understand why you would tell the folks out
there that he murdered a federal officer."

But after Oklahoma City, the vacant-headed notion
that popped up in the minds of many media persons
like thistle after an early springtime rain held that
Randy Weaver was in some way related to that fearsome
mob of neo-revolutionists who were lurking out there
somewhere and who were responsible for the bombing, radical crazies who were joined at the mind's hip

in a fearsome underground conspiracy fanned by a common wind of hatred against the government. And this idea led, as if in step, to the conclusion that everyone who had ever expressed enmity of one kind or another against the government were likely of the same criminal ilk as the bombers in Oklahoma City, whoever they were, and therefore Randy Weaver must somehow be connected to them, if not in fact, then in spirit.

Ideas can be as criminal as criminals. Ideas can be vicious and evil and lurk on the borders of reason, and they can strike the innocent. Almost immediately this outlaw of an idea began to ply its poisonous stuff; that is the idea that any who were distressed with the government in the past were to now be viewed as suspect, as the dangerous element within. President Clinton, seeking to be seen at last as a resolute and timely leader, promised the nation that the bombers would be arrested forthwith. Then he led the nation's New Inquisition by suggesting that all of that mean talk from the far right where his most vocal enemies lay had probably encouraged renegades such as the Oklahoma bombers to do their evil deed. And those who called themselves Constitutionalists, and Tax Protesters, and people who called themselves "Patriots" and those who were members of "The Militia," and many other fringes on *both* the right and the left became the victims of the new paranoia.

Waco was even more in the news than the Weaver case as the media tied the Oklahoma City bombing to the second anniversary date of the Waco holocaust, in which nineteen children and scores of adults were burned to cinders. But the "Waco crazies" were cultist, were they not? The Branch Davidians had resisted the federal officers and several federal officers themselves had been killed, which seemed to lessen the tragedy that innocent children had been burned alive like baby lambs on fiery spits. No one spoke, not Ms. Reno, the Attorney General, not anyone, about how you could hear the screams of the little children through the flames, and how the smell of burning children had stifled the air and spoiled American history.

I was on *Larry King Live* the night of the Oklahoma City bombing. Already the gun-control folks were trying to make a connection on that show as strained as the connection was between the bombers, whoever they were, and those who had fought against gun control. The idea was that a clandestine voluntary militia was arming itself to do us in, and a national consensus seemed to have already formed—that the Oklahoma City bombers were a part of a well-armed militia, a gigantic conspiracy, and it followed, therefore, that in order to fight the militia and to make America safe from bombers, we must have gun control.

The irresponsible rumors that surrounded the Weaver case had also done its disservice to my very good friend, Larry King, who turned to me, he in Washington and I in New York City. By the magic of satellite Larry said something like the others on television had said—something to the effect that I had defended Randy Weaver, who had killed a federal officer, and what Larry wanted to know was whether this murder was connected to the same right-wing weirdos who must be responsible for the Oklahoma horror? After I corrected Larry in the way that one corrects a good friend, and after the show was over, I realized that out of every thousand people who had heard his question containing the accusation of murder, some lesser number had not heard my correction, some probably having gone to answer the phone about then or to take the pizza out of the oven, and some may have even turned to another station—I hope not—before my answer was given, and some, having heard my answer, must still believe that Randy was guilty, because, after all, this guy on *Larry King* was Weaver's lawyer, and you know lawyers, and besides, this Weaver was a crazy who stored up a boxcar full of guns and ammunition and was a racist and had screwy religious beliefs, and a federal officer had been killed, and Weaver was charged by the government, so he must be guilty. That is how some of us, not you, not I, not Larry King, think, this "where-there's-smoke-there's-fire" syndrome, and that is why, in part, these false rumors that Randy Weaver murdered a federal officer have so long persisted, even after the evidence was clear and crisp to the contrary.

I told Larry King that night that we had to be careful. These are dangerous times. When we are afraid, we want to be protected, and since we cannot protect ourselves against such horrors as mass murder by bombers, we are tempted to run to the government, a government that is always willing to trade the promise of protection for our freedom, which left, as always, the question: How much freedom are we willing to relinquish for such a bald promise?

Already the President was calling for more power, more power for the FBI. He wanted a thousand more men. And he wanted to use the army, no less, in situations like Oklahoma City. And he wanted more power to tap our phones and to invade our privacy. He wanted express authority from Congress to infiltrate the fringe groups and, in short, to snoop and to peer and to spy on the citizenry, especially on those who hold different beliefs from those that flow in the phlegmatic and murky mainstream of America. But the question remains, will we really be safer with a thousand more, or a hundred thousand more FBI agents armed with even greater power to more easily tap our phones that are already so easily tapped and to break into our homes that are no longer safe under the much-mangled exclusionary rule?

In answer to that question, the Randy Weaver trial began to take on new and deeper meaning, for although I had accepted Randy's defense under the circumstances and for the reasons you will discover in Chapter 1, it was not until the trial was over, and as a result of the Oklahoma City bombing, that I first began to understand what the full significance of the Weaver case had been. For that reason, I have added a new chapter, the one I have entitled "The Trial of Randy Weaver: The Tyranny of Government," in which I recount the facts of the trial itself as seen from my viewpoint as the chief trial attorney who defended Randy Weaver.

And out of the story of this trial, like distant prophetic words from the firmament, emerges a wise and warning voice. We must listen to this voice, a voice often muffled by the shock and anger and fear we suffer as the products of that Oklahoma horror. In order that we may better hear this voice and understand its message I have chosen to include in this edition, and for the first time, the story of the Randy Weaver trial as I tried it and as I lived it.

*May 26, 1995*
*Jackson, Wyoming*

*Writing a book about a lofty subject such as freedom* is like trying to jump from rock to rock across the creek without getting your feet wet. No matter how you plan your course, you are likely to slip off into the water somewhere. The choice, of course, is whether one wishes to stay on the bank with dry feet, or take the risk of wet feet to get to the other side.

Doctors called upon to attend the sick cannot prescribe a cure unless they are first able to diagnose the illness. Even before that, they must detect that the patient is ill. In the case of our freedoms, I can confidently say the patient is in grave danger. Having said so, and should you agree in whole or in part, we have, together, taken the first step toward the cure.

As for solutions, there are only two kinds—those from outside the self and those from within. The first suggests that we destroy our enemies, that we manipulate or neutralize them, that we discover detours around them, that we suffer their impositions against us, or, at last, that we even love them. In any event, the solution acknowledges the existence of outside forces that deter our progress and impede our happiness. On the other hand, there persists the idea—one with which I am in agreement—that solutions are mainly matters of the self, that power vested in others is often irrelevant to our freedom, that the only change essential for the betterment of the human condition is to *change within,* that we are the fountainhead of power, and that, therefore, we need not free the world—we need only free ourselves. Yet I have never been an exclusionist. It makes no more sense to argue that all solutions should fall into one category or the other than to argue that a mustard plaster is the proper remedy for every ailment.

The problem, however, is not so much in finding solutions as in making the solutions work. Any splinter can cause a fatal infection. This being so, one also knows one can never detect all the splinters that make up the smoothest stick. Marx, for example, hated the exploitation of the masses, but his solutions, however corrupted in their application, resulted in the enslavement of whole nations. Christ also had a good idea—that we love one another. But his followers, attempting to realize his simple, perhaps perfect remedy, disagreed on what they thought were crucial points—whether they should hold their meetings on Saturday or Sunday—whether members of the flock at baptism should be nearly drowned to wash away their sins, or whether a few drops of water on the head would suffice. In the end, his followers proved to be strong on organization, unsurpassed on dogma, supreme on sophistry, but not much on love. They fought endless wars in his name, murdered hordes of the innocent, burned countless women at the stake as witches, bashed in the heads of "heathen" Indian children, and left the world riddled with guilt and fear.

Freedom in America, as bountiful and precious as it is, has always been a strange conglomerate of the divine and the fanciful. Understanding freedom in America is like listening to a one-armed piano player. His one arm performs not only its assigned task, but has painfully attempted to undertake the function of the missing limb. He plays the melody with the magnificent frills and rolls of the virtuoso. He represents all of the higher virtues of the species: He is resourceful, creative, vigorous, and he is very brave. In listening, our minds provide for us what our ears do not—the music of the other hand. But after we assess his performance, as admirable as it has been, we know that something is, indeed, missing.

Freedom in America works best for those who can afford it. As the fellow said in *The Grapes of Wrath*, "You're just as free as you've got Jack to pay for it." It is not as much an idea as it is a commodity. It is not as much a liberated state of being as it is an item on the shelf that, along with the purchaser, may be purchased. It is not as much a right as a component of commerce.

The danger, of course, is that we have become the purchasers of the fable of freedom. When we vigorously argue to our neighbors that Americans are free, our neighbors will likely assert that they "buy" that. Having *bought* the fable, it belongs to us, and we fight to keep it like howling apes protecting their trinkets and their tinfoil.

On the other hand, some of us enjoy a state of freedom that never enters even the dreams of those in many other cultures. I sit warm and comfortably at my desk recording these thoughts. My stomach is full—too full. I do not fear intrusions from brown-shirted agents of the government. If I make minimal efforts at compliance with the rules that preserve the power structure, I will likely be left alone, even if I criticize the power structure. I am essentially free to rant and rave and to emit all manner of noxious noise. It is this dichotomy that serves as both our pride and our poison.

Today there are, as indeed, there have always been, insidious, enslaving forces at work in America. Today's emerging tyranny emanates from a New King, from a nonliving power center composed at its core of monolithic corporate entities encased and protected by endless layers of governmental bureaucracies. The primary strategy of the New King is to convert all rights, all human energy, all goals and, at last, all humans into fungible commodities, for the New King exists solely for commerce and its life's blood, its green blood, its money—and its singular mission is profit. The New King's principal means of control is the media that sells us the myths of freedom, that, when we doubt, reassures us we are free, and that programs us and our children to accept the notion that all human function, all human desires, indeed, even immortality itself can, at last, be satisfied at the marketplace.

I am not against religion—nor am I against commerce. I am, however, reluctant to offer solutions. If the Church has anything to do with it, those who offer solutions outside the scriptures will be condemned to eternal hell. If government has anything to do with them, any sound idea will be consumed in the bureaucracy, and if the idea should somehow escape the grinding teeth of its machinery, the author will be labeled an enemy of the state and disemboweled in one fashion or another. If corporate America has anything to do with it, any ideas that threaten its power will be branded as leftist, or commie, or un-American, and the author of such reform banished as a heretic against the most sacred of all religions in America, Free Enterprise.

At last, I have tired of the issue as well as these arguments. If this collection of free-floating thoughts about freedom is to have any efficacy, it will come from freely saying what is on my mind, saying it as well as I can, saying it in such a way that satisfies me, or even amuses me; and if a solution seems to appear, well, why not give it recognition? It does no one any good bouncing around in the mind's soupy fog where, in all probability, it will eventually be cast into the trash pile of the magnificent and the forgotten. And if no solutions seem at hand, well, I was never born to solve all of the world's problems, and those who tried were either fools or martyrs.

Sometimes it is easier for a poor man to tolerate his corns than to go barefoot and discard the shoes that cause them. Despite the existence of sharp rocks and cockleburs, there is something magical about a boy's barefoot freedom. If only we could convince the world's leaders not to walk in each other's shoes but, instead, to meet and to talk to each other in their bare feet; likely, the people, as well as the earth, would benefit immensely. I think, therefore, I shall walk barefooted herein. I think I shall walk wherever my feet will take me. I hope you'll come too.

*Gerry Spence*
*Jackson Hole, Wyoming*
*July 4, 1993*

*Although we give lip service to the notion of freedom, we know the government is no longer the servant of the people but, at last, has become the people's master. We have stood by like timid sheep while the wolf killed—first the weak, then the strays, then those on the outer edges of the flock, until at last the entire flock belonged to the wolf.*

# 1

# THE EYE OF THE WOLF

## *The*

## *Tyranny*

## *of*

## *Justice*

*Randy Weaver's wife was dead, shot through the head while* she clutched her child to her breast. His son was shot, twice. First they shot the child's arm—probably destroyed the arm. The child cried out. Then, as the boy was running, they shot him in the back. Randy Weaver himself had been shot and wounded and Kevin Harris, a kid the Weavers had all but adopted, was dying of a chest wound. The blood hadn't cooled on Ruby Hill before the national media announced that I had taken the defense of Randy Weaver. Then all hell broke loose. My sister wrote me decrying my defense of this "racist." There were letters to the editors in several papers that expressed their disappointment that I would lend my services to a person with Weaver's beliefs. And I received a letter from my close friend, Alan Hirschfield, the former chairman and chief executive officer of Columbia Pictures and Twentieth-Century Fox, imploring me to withdraw. He wrote:

After much thought I decided to write this letter to you. It represents a very profound concern on my part regarding your decision to represent Randy Weaver. While I applaud and fully understand your motives in taking such a case, I nonetheless find this individual defense troubling. It is so because of the respectability and credibility your involvement imparts to a cause which I find despicable.

The Aryan Nation, The Brotherhood and the Order are all groups dedicated to only one premise—hatred of the unlike by the like. They deny the Holocaust and preach the gospel of ethnic debasement and racist supremacy. They are societal malcontents and misfits who espouse nothing worthwhile. It is the beliefs of these groups that Mr. Weaver represents.

Mr. Hirschfield went on to argue that my involvement would lend dignity to an illicit and repugnant movement:

This is not Huey Newton and the Black Panthers fighting 200 years of prejudice and second class citizenship nor even the PLO seeking a homeland by terrorist methods. While I abhor terrorism of any kind I do understand its politics. Not so with the philosophy of the groups Mr. Weaver stands for.

The issues involved are reminiscent of the recent national uproar over the Warner Brothers recording made by the rap singer Ice T which advocated killing cops. Other tracks on the CD were virulently anti-semitic and homophobic. The right of Ice T to publicly record these songs was not the issue. What *was* troublesome to myself and others was the role of Warner Bros. in disseminating his message in the name of preserving their "creative integrity." I gave an interview on this subject and suggested that at least in business there was a line to be drawn between unbridled creative freedom and corporate responsibility. In Warner's case they could have chosen not to distribute this record (it still would have found a distributor), instead they trumpeted the creative freedom argument and by lending their world renowned prestige to the issue they imparted to Ice T and his message a legitimacy wholly undeserved and in doing so made the recording a national hit in contrast to his previous mediocre results.

My premise, therefore, is not the right of Weaver or anyone else to the best possible defense but rather the message sent when the finest trial lawyer in America undertakes that defense, simply to make that point. The message, I believe, will embolden those espousing the cause Weaver represents and encourage other mindless haters to join up. The resultant media attention will provide a platform previously never enjoyed by these people.

I clearly know this is not your intent in defending Mr. Weaver but I believe ... there *is* a time when a person of your extraordinary talent and commitment, and knowing full well the notoriety that comes with your representation, perhaps demurs, rather than allow your prominent and respected persona to add legitimacy and notoriety to a sick and twisted philosophy.

As you know, I am not a religious person ... but I am keenly conscious of my heritage and the endless persecution Jews throughout the world have suffered. There is in my mind no worse group of people than those involved here who espouse both hatred and violence against Jews, blacks and other minorities without any purpose other than hatred itself. They don't seek a homeland, they don't propose alternatives and they don't want a solution other than the one Hitler sought. As a result of your involvement these same people will be given a greatly expanded voice at this trial.

It is because of this that I write and ask you to reconsider your decision to involve yourself in this case. I do so out of total respect and personal affection for you. And, of course, whatever your decision you will always have the same respect and that same affection from me.

Your friend,
*Alan J. Hirschfield*

The next morning I delivered the following by carrier to Mr. Hirschfield:

I cherish your letter. It reminds me once again of our friendship, for only friends can speak and hear each other in matters so deeply a part of the soul. And your letter reminds me as well, as we must all be reminded, of the unspeakable pain every Jew has suffered from the horrors of the Holocaust. No better evidence of our friendship could be shown than your intense caring concerning what I do and what I stand for.

I met Randy Weaver in jail on the evening of his surrender. His eyes had no light in them. He was unshaven and dirty. He was naked except for yellow plastic prison coveralls, and he was cold. His small feet were clad in rubber prison sandals. In the stark setting of the prison conference room he seemed diminutive and fragile. He had spent eleven days and nights in a standoff against the government, and he had lost. His wife was dead. His son was dead. His friend was near death. Weaver himself had been wounded. He had lost his freedom. He had lost it all. And now he stood face to face with a stranger who towered over him and whose words were not words of comfort. When I spoke, you, Alan, were on my mind.

"My name is Gerry Spence," I began. "I'm the lawyer you've been told about. Before we begin to talk I want you to understand that I do not share any of your political or religious beliefs. Many of my dearest friends are Jews. My daughter is married to a Jew. My sister is married to a black man. She has adopted a black child. I deplore what the Nazis stand for. If I defend you I will not defend your political beliefs or your religious beliefs, but your rights as an American citizen to a fair trial." His quiet answer was, "That is all I ask." Then I motioned him to a red plastic chair and I took a similar one. And as the guards marched by and from time to time peered in, he told his story.

Alan, you are a good and fair man. That I know. Were it otherwise we would not be such friends. Yet it is your pain I hear most clearly—exacerbated, I know, by the fact that your friend should represent your enemy. Yet what drew me to this case was my own pain. Let me tell you the facts.

Randy Weaver's principal crime against the government had been his failure to appear in court on a charge of possessing illegal firearms. The first crime was not his. He had been entrapped—intentionally, systematically, patiently, purposely entrapped—by a federal agent who solicited him to cut off, contrary to federal law, the barrels of a couple of shotguns. Randy Weaver never owned an illegal weapon in his life. He was not engaged in the manufacture of illegal weapons. The idea of selling an illegal firearm had never entered his mind until the government agent suggested it and encouraged him to act illegally. The government knew he needed the money. He is as poor as an empty cupboard. He had three daughters, a son and a wife to support. He lived in a small house in the woods without electricity or running water. Although he is a small, frail man, with tiny, delicate hands who probably weighs no more than a hundred twenty pounds, he made an honest living by chopping firewood and by seasonal work as a logger.

This man is wrong. His beliefs are wrong. His relationship to mankind is wrong. He was perhaps legally wrong when he failed to appear and defend himself in court. But the first wrong was not his. Nor was the first wrong the government's. The first wrong was ours.

In this country we embrace the myth that we are still a democracy when we know that we are not a democracy, that we are not free, that the government does not serve us but subjugates us. Although we give lip service to the notion of freedom, we know the government is no longer the servant of the people but, at last, has become the people's master. We have stood by like timid sheep while the wolf killed—first the weak, then the strays, then those on the outer edges of the flock, until at last the entire flock belonged to the wolf. We did not care about the weak or about the strays. They were not a part of the flock. We did not care about those on the outer edges. They had chosen to be there. But as the wolf worked its way toward the center of the flock we discovered that we were now on the outer edges. Now we must look the wolf squarely in the eye. That we did not do so when the first of us was ripped and torn and eaten was the first wrong. It was our wrong.

That none of us have felt responsible for having lost our freedom has been a part of an insidious progression. In the beginning the attention of the flock was directed not to the marauding wolf but to our own deviant members within the flock. We rejoiced when the wolf destroyed them for they were our enemies. We were told that the weak lay under the rocks while we faced the blizzards to rustle our food, and we did not care when the wolf took them. We argued that they deserved it. When one of our flock faced the wolf alone it was always eaten. Each of us was afraid of the wolf, but as a flock we were not afraid. Indeed, the wolf cleansed the herd by destroying the weak and dismembering the aberrant element within. As time went by, strangely the herd felt more secure under the rule of the wolf. It believed that by belonging to this wolf it would remain safe from all the other wolves. But we were eaten just the same.

No one knows better than children of the Holocaust how the lessons of history must never be forgotten. Yet Americans, whose battle cry was once, "Give me liberty or give me death," have sat placidly by as a new king was crowned. In America a new king was crowned by the shrug of our shoulders when our neighbors were wrongfully seized. A new king was crowned when we capitulated to a regime that was no longer sensitive to people but to non-people— to corporations, to money and to power. The new king was crowned when we turned our heads as the poor and the forgotten and the damned were rendered mute and defenseless, not because they were evil but because, in the scheme of our lives, they seemed unimportant, not because they were essentially dangerous but because they were essentially powerless. The new king was crowned when we cheered the government on as it prosecuted the progeny of our ghettos and filled our prisons with black men whose first crime was that they were born in the ghettos. We cheered the new king on as it diluted our right to be secure in our homes against unlawful searches and secure in the courts against unlawful evidence. We cheered the new king on because we were told that our sacred rights were but "loopholes" by which our enemies, the murderers and rapists and thieves and drug dealers, escaped. We were told that those who fought for our rights, the lawyers, were worse than the thieves who stole from us in the night, that our juries were irresponsible and ignorant and ought not be trusted. We watched with barely more than a mumble as the legal system that once protected us became populated with judges who were appointed by the new king. At last the new king was crowned when we forgot the lessons of history, that *when the rights of our enemies have been wrested from them, our own rights have been lost as well, for the same rights serve both citizen and criminal.*

When Randy Weaver failed to appear in court because he had lost his trust in the government we witnessed the fruit of our crime. The government, indeed, had no intent to protect his rights. The government had but one purpose, as it remains today, the disengagement of this citizen from society. Those who suffered and died in the Holocaust must have exquisitely understood such illicit motivations of power.

I have said that I was attracted to the case out of my own pain. Let me tell you the facts: A crack team of trained government marksmen sneaked on to Randy Weaver's small isolated acreage on a reconnaissance mission preparatory to a contemplated arrest. They wore camouflage suits and were heavily armed. They gave Randy no warning of their coming. They came without a warrant. They never identified themselves.

The Weavers owned three dogs, two small crossbred collie mutts and a yellow lab, a big pup a little over a year old whose most potent weapon was his tail with which he could beat a full-grown man to death. The dog, Striker, was a close member of the Weaver family. Not only was he a companion for the children, but in the winter he pulled the family sled to haul their water supply from the spring below. When the dogs discovered the intruders, they raised a ruckus, and Randy, his friend, Kevin, and Randy's fourteen year old son, Sam, grabbed their guns and followed the dogs to investigate.

When the government agents were confronted with the barking dog, they did what men who have been taught to kill do. They shot Striker. The boy, barely larger than a ten year old child, heard his dog's yelp, saw the dog fall dead, and, as a fourteen year old might, he returned the fire. Then the government agents shot the child in the arm. He turned and ran, the arm flopping, and when he did the officers, still unidentified as such, shot the child in the back and killed him.

Kevin Harris witnessed the shooting of the dog. Then he saw Sam being shot as the boy turned and ran. To Kevin there was no alternative. He knew if he ran these intruders, whoever they were, would kill him as well. In defense of himself, he raised his rifle and shot in the direction of the officer who had killed the boy. Then while the agents were in disarray, Kevin retreated to the Weaver cabin.

In the meantime Randy Weaver had been off in another direction and had only heard the shooting, the dog's yelp and the gunfire that followed. Randy hollered for his son and shot his shotgun in the air to attract the boy.

"Come on home, Sam. Come home."

Over and over again he called.

Finally he heard the boy call back. "I'm comin', Dad." Those were the last words he ever heard from his son.

Later the same day Randy, Kevin and Vicki Weaver, Randy's wife, went down to where the boy lay and carried his body back to an outbuilding near their cabin. There they removed the child's clothing and bathed his wounds and prepared the body. The next evening Weaver's oldest daughter, Sarah, sixteen, Kevin and Randy went back to the shed to have a last look at Sam. When they did, government snipers opened fire. Randy was hit in the shoulder. The three turned and ran for the house where Vicki, with her ten month old baby in her arms stood holding the door open. As the three entered the house Vicki was shot and slowly fell to her knees, her head resting on the floor like one kneeling in prayer. Randy ran up and took the baby that she clutched, and then he lifted his wife's head. Half of her face was blown away.

Kevin was also hit. Huge areas of muscle in his arm were blown out, and his lung was punctured in several places. Randy and his sixteen-year-old daughter stretched the dead mother on the floor of the cabin and covered her with a blanket where she remained for over eight days as the siege progressed.

By this time there were officers by the score, troops, armored personnel carriers, helicopters, radios, televisions, robots, and untold armaments surrounding the little house. I will not burden you with the misery and horror the family suffered in the standoff. I will tell you that finally Bo Gritz, Randy's former commander in the Special Forces, came to help in the negotiations. Gritz told Randy that if he would surrender, Gritz would guarantee him a fair trial, and before the negotiations were ended, Randy came to the belief that I would represent him. Although Gritz had contacted me before he spoke to Randy, I had only agreed to talk to Randy. But the accuracy of what was said between Gritz and me and what was heard by Randy somehow got lost in the horror, and Randy's belief that I would represent him if he surrendered was, in part, his motivation for finally submitting to arrest.

And so my friend, Alan, you can now understand the pain I feel in this case. It is pain that comes from the realization that we have permitted a government to act in our name and on our behalf in this criminal fashion. It is the pain of watching the government as it now attempts to lie about its criminal complicity in this affair and to cover its crimes by charging Randy with crimes he did not commit, including murder. It is the pain of seeing an innocent woman with her child in her arms murdered and innocent children subjected to these atrocities. Indeed, as a human being, I feel Randy's irrepressible pain and horror and grief.

I also feel your pain, my friend. Yet I know that in the end, if you were the judge at the trial of Adolph Eichmann, you would have insisted that he not have ordinary counsel, but the best counsel. In the same way, if you were the judge in Randy's case, and you had the choice, I have no doubt that despite your own pain you might well have appointed me to defend him. In the end you would know that the Holocaust must never stand for part justice, or average justice, but for the most noble of ideals—that even the enemies of the Jews themselves must receive the best justice the system can provide. If it were otherwise the meaning of the Holocaust would be accordingly besmirched.

Alan, I agree with your arguments. They are proper and they are true. I agree that my defense of Randy Weaver may attach a legitimacy and dignity to his politics and religion. But it may, as well, stand for the proposition that there are those who do not condone this kind of criminal action by our government. I view the defense of Randy Weaver's case as an opportunity to address a more vital issue, one that transcends a white separatist movement or notions of the supremacy of one race over another, for the ultimate enemy of any people is not the angry hate groups that fester within, but a government itself that has lost its respect for the individual. The ultimate enemy of democracy is not the drug dealer or the crooked politician or the crazed skinhead. The ultimate enemy is the New King that has become so powerful it can murder its own citizens with impunity.

To the same extent that Randy Weaver cannot find justice in this country we, too, will be deprived of justice. At last, my defense of Randy Weaver is a defense for every Jew and every Gentile, for every black and every gay who loves freedom and deplores tyranny.

Although I understand that it will be easy for my defense of Randy Weaver to be confused with an endorsement of the politics of the Aryan Nation, my challenge will be to demonstrate that we can still be a nation where the rights of the individual, despite his race, color or religion, remain supreme. If this be not so, then we are all lost. If this is not so, it is because we have forgotten the lessons of our histories—the history of the American Revolution as well as the history of the Holocaust.

And so my friend, Alan, if I were to withdraw from the defense of Randy Weaver as you request, I would be required to abandon my belief that this system has any remaining virtue. I would be more at fault than the federal government that has murdered these people for I have not been trained to murder but to defend. I would be less of a man than my client who had the courage of his convictions. I would lose all respect for myself. I would be unable to any longer be your friend, for friendship must always have its foundation in respect. Therefore as my friend, I ask that you not require this of me. I ask, instead, for your prayers, your understanding and your continued love.

As ever,

*Gerry Spence*
*Jackson Hole, Wyoming*

11

# 2

# THE TRIAL OF RANDY WEAVER

*The*

*Tyranny*

*of*

*Government*

*This account of Randy Weaver's trial is dedicated to the memory of Vicki Weaver, Randy's devoted wife, and to Sammy, his small, brave son. From the deaths of Vicki and Sammy may we learn and remember important lessons in this blessed and perpetual business of freedom.*

*Ronald D. Howen, the Assistant United States Attorney, a* powerful, square-jawed, humorless man, had attempted from the earliest moments of the trial to convict Randy Weaver by tying him to the Aryan Nations with slim circumstantial strings. Everyone knew the Aryan Nations as a miserable conglomerate of discontents, who like fanged sheep, followed Pastor Richard Butler of the "Church of Jesus Christ Christian." Butler preached that the "Nations" were composed of the twelve lost tribes of Israel, which were, of course, all white and all "cleansed of Jews." Blacks were the descendants of Cain, and the unfortunate mixtures of blacks and whites Butler ignobly labeled, "Mongrels." Blacks had been stricken black in punishment for their inherited sin, the eternal libel born of the Cain and

Abel legend, and, therefore, according to Butler, a natural enmity persisted between "the children of Satan, the Negroes and the children of The Most High God, Yahweh," who were, according to this logic, the divine citizens of the Aryan Nations.

Pastor Butler preached to his flock in the Church of Jesus Christ Christian in Idaho, and the sermons were not of the universal love of Christ, but the tirades of universal hatred, a sort of genetic malevolence against all who were not white, especially the Jew, who Butler, by the abracadabra of his fanaticism, transformed into a subspecies of the hated non-white. "We believe that the Canaanite Jew is the natural enemy of our White Christian Race. This is attested by scripture and all secular history. The Jew is like a destroying virus that attacks our racial body to destroy our White culture and the purity of our Race. Those of our Race who resist these attacks are called 'chosen and faithful.' "

The twelve lost tribes were identified by Pastor Butler as Denmark, Norway, Finland, Germany, France, Italy, Holland, Spain, Iceland, Great Britain, and Sweden, with the United States and Canada being considered as one, thus causing the arithmetic to come out right—the twelve, not thirteen, lost tribes.

History? Well, according to Butler, history is only the work of the devil. God's history, as revealed to Butler, was the only true history, and to know such history one need be no scholar. One need only read the Bible and listen to God, and, accordingly, to Pastor Butler who would faithfully reveal the word of God.

The goal of the Aryan Nations was twofold: first, to preserve the white race, one of the "twelve foundation stones for the redemption of our Aryan Racial Nation" being "the recognition that an Aryan National State is an institution that has a single duty to itself and the people of the Racial Nation; the preservation of the Race . . . and that a nation begins and ends as a race, and everything else is predicated upon this fact." The second goal of the Nation was the elimination of all Jews and the confiscation of all property held by Jews (as well as other "non-whites"). Under the Platform for the Aryan National State, only Aryans were allowed citizenship. Only citizens could vote, conduct business, possess and bear arms, hold office in government, industry or society, and only these citizens—the Aryan whites—could belong to the military or law enforcement. Whites would be free of all taxation except a voluntary ten percent tithe upon net increase in wealth over the previous year. Whites could receive loans without interest charges. Non-citizens could visit in the republic, but only under the custodianship of a citizen.

The platform provided, "All hybrids called Jews are to be repatriated from the Republic's territory, all their wealth to be redistributed to restore our people, and it shall be a capital offense to advocate or promote Jew Talmudic anti-Christ Communism"—whatever that meant—"in any manner or any other crimes against nature."

Under the constitution of the Aryan Nations, "A credible news media is to be established for the betterment of the people by: (1) Requiring all editors, writers, actors, broadcasters, and all having any part in the media to be citizens; (2) Not allowing the circulation of non-white media except by permission of the government, and then only with appropriate comments from an Aryan cultural viewpoint; (3) Forbidding the publication, broadcasting, televising or circulation of any material which is not conducive to the National welfare."

The cult had often been labeled neo-Nazi, and these so-called skinheads with their shaved skulls, black shirts and swastikas had gathered at Ruby Ridge to maintain their "vigil" during the Weaver standoff. Although Colonel Bo Gritz had assured me that Randy Weaver was not a member of the Aryan Nations, and, indeed, he was not, Weaver nevertheless had candidly displayed an occasional trapping and employed, from time to time, some of their Biblical language.

It is easy for us to hate these truants from reason who propose ideas that insult the dignity of the species, ideas that harbor a self-contained hypocrisy. I, too, had begun to hate those who were diseased with the disease of hatred. During the trial I often remembered the earlier arguments of my friend, Alan Hirschfield. In important ways he was right. Involuntarily I had become the hero of many whose causes and creeds were antithetical to my own. Yet the same pesky voice pestered in my ear. If we do not preserve the right of our enemies to worship and to speak as they please, our own preachments of freedom are as empty as empty cans on the beach.

And Assistant United States Attorney, Ronald D. Howen, was also stricken by the same hatred of hatred, by an enmity that, untethered, could lead to the prosecution of people, not for alleged crimes, but for their loathsome beliefs. And, as the trial proceeded, Howen's case against Randy Weaver proved to be as minuscule as his abhorrence of Randy Weaver was towering. I had argued to Judge Edward Lodge that Randy Weaver was not a member of the Aryan Nations, for in truth, he was flat against belonging to anything—not the NRA, not the PTA, not the Boy Scouts, not even the local garden club. He was a separatist. But, I argued, even if he did belong to the Aryan Nations, his membership in that or any other organization could not be considered as evidence of his having committed any crime. One is not guilty of murder because one belongs to a church that preaches hatred of one who has been murdered.

But Howen vowed to the judge that he would tie Randy Weaver's beliefs to his actions. Based on that assurance, Judge Lodge permitted evidence to the effect that Randy and Vicki spoke of the coming of Christ, of Armageddon when the world would be filled with agony and turmoil and the federal government would be peopled with evil officers who would attack innocent citizens. And Howen was successful as well in dragging before the jury many of the repugnant tenets of the Aryan Nations, including their hatred of blacks and Jews.

Earlier, through hearsay testimony, Howen had told the Weaver grand jury that members of the Order, an activist group in some way connected with The Church of Jesus Christ Christian, had bombed the house of a priest, attacked gays, robbed armored cars and committed murder. Through these witnesses he told the grand jury that members of the Order even lived in the same town as the jurors themselves, just down the street as a matter of fact, and the grand jury should indict Randy Weaver for the very safety of all of the town's citizens.

Entwining Randy into the web of guilt by implication, Howen displayed to the jury an Aryan Nations belt buckle, widely sold at gun shows and swap meets, one that Randy supposedly wore. He held up pictures for the jury to see, showing Randy with his hair closely clipped in the style of the skinheads, and, thereby, he asked the jury to conclude that Randy Weaver, like the skinheads, must be one who hates federal officers, who stores up guns and ammunition for the purpose of killing federal officers, and, therefore, who must have intended to kill Marshal Degan or at least plotted to kill him as part of an evil conspiracy. And when I asked who the members of the conspiracy were, I was told they were Randy, his wife and his children, Kevin Harris and others. I wondered in open court how Elisheba, ten months of age, and little Rachel, then barely 10 years old, could be members of a criminal conspiracy, but when I raised this question, I was attacked by Howen for making light of the serious business of the criminal law.

As the trial dragged on, Howen painted an evil portrait of Randy Weaver—a vicious, wild-eyed radical, who had plotted from the beginning, even before he and his family had migrated to Idaho, to instigate a violent confrontation with federal authorities. He had stored up hundreds of thousands of rounds of ammunition for this purpose and he owned a score of guns or more, all of which Owen had hauled into the courtroom and stacked up in a huge pile before the jury. The floor space in front of the jury box looked like the best part of an army ordnance depot by the time the deputies had finished carrying in the evil evidence. But the guns and the ammunition had been legally purchased. And, when purchased, there was no law against Randy Weaver possessing as many guns and as much ammunition as he chose to own.

From time to time, I would look over at this little man who sat beside me at the counsel table in his one gray suit with his small, tentative smile, and displaying his brave good humor. Weaver often offered his kind salutations to the marshals who, every day, sat sullenly, silently, behind him with loaded pistols. And when I looked into his eyes and heard his simple words I saw that he was afraid, and sometimes confused, but that always he trusted me, and always he denied that he had ever been a member of the Aryan Nations. "I attended a couple of their picnics during the summer, but I never joined them. Their beliefs were different than mine."

I then thought of the story my mother told me as a child, about the swan who played with the crows and who was caught one day in the farmer's net along with the crows. The farmer, my mother's story went, intended to kill the crows because they were eating his corn crop, but the swan begged to be set free. "Obviously I am not a crow," the swan argued. "Anyone can see that." But the farmer said, "You must be a crow, for you were caught with them." And thereafter the farmer killed all who had been trapped in his net. "And so," my mother would counsel, "be careful who you choose as friends."

During my lifetime, we in America have often endured the invidious reasoning that seeks to prove guilt by associating people with unpopular causes: the internment of innocent and patriotic Japanese in my own home state of Wyoming during World War II; the McCarthy inquisitions when decent people were smeared with the taint of Communism; and the frightening times during the Vietnam war when good citizens were vilified as traitors, even shot and killed, as at Kent State, should they protest a war with which they disagreed. And after the Oklahoma bombing in April of 1995, we were told that the FBI was investigating individuals as bombing suspects that included such circumstances as: "He [the suspect] would make remarks, like how we were losing our freedom . . ." which would likely qualify every thinking, peace-loving American as a bombing suspect, and "the suspect liked to wear military fatigues, was anti-government, and had a fascination with firearms," which could cast millions into the irredeemable trough of suspicion.

I had grown up believing the police were just good people like Andy Sutka, the policeman who lived next door and who, my parents told me, would come to find me when I was lost, or who would help me when I needed help. I never saw Andy Sutka without a big smile on his face, and I saw him every day, and his kids were my pals. We went fishing for perch together at the slew and played marbles and wrestled on the lawn. And at night I would lie in bed with my pillow against my open upstairs bedroom window, and the sounds of Andy plunking his guitar and the whole family singing those old country westerns would drift up to me in the sweet, soft summer air.

We all have our primary experiences by which we judge the people and the events of our lives. As I grew older I naturally thought of the police, yes, even the federal police, as folks like Andy Sutka. They were decent folks who lived next door to decent folks. They were trustworthy, loyal, helpful, friendly

. . . they were adult Boy Scouts who carried a badge and a sidearm.

But over the years, as a criminal defense attorney, my in-court experiences with the police forced me to the realization that police, like the rest of us, want to win. We are a competitive people who, from the earliest times, have donned a jersey of one color or another, and we have been taught that we should fight for that color jersey, and win. Many police, perhaps most, struggle under the misguided belief that when the accused is guilty it becomes the duty of the police to see that the accused is convicted and punished. Many police seem to weigh one wrong against the other—their own wrong of fiddling with the evidence, of intentionally omitting exculpatory facts, even the criminal wrong of planting or manufacturing evidence or, equally reprehensible, lying under oath, against what many police see as the greater wrong of permitting the guilty to escape his just dues. Indeed, the argument that it is all right for the police to cheat if, in the process, they catch the criminal, is commonly dramatized in the movies and on the television screen. This idea, in fact, is applauded by many a citizen as justice in the raw without all the bothersome loopholes that permit the guilty to escape. On the screen we often witness the cop blithely picking the lock of a suspect's home and illegally entering and searching his room. We watch the illegal phone tap being made or the cop, the hero, smashing a witness up against the wall and brutally pounding information out of the hapless creature, and we cheer him on.

At the same time, many years in the courtroom have taught me that most police officers cannot withstand a powerful, well-prepared cross-examination. Often they react. Often they display their anger, sometimes they reveal a dark underside, and then juries will reject their testimony. A good cross-examination can usually expose the holes in their investigation, their errors, perhaps even their wrongdoing. The police, as

I have grown to know them in the hard, tough world of the courtroom, are far different from the Andy Sutkas of my childhood. The police have become fair game and, indeed, they ought to be. Were it otherwise we would need no laws, no rules, no trials and no juries. The police, as in every police state, would simply level their charges and lead the defendant to his blindfolded stance before the firing squad. During Randy Weaver's trial, an agony for him that he endured for nearly three months, I found the minions of the law—the special agents of the FBI—to be men who proved themselves not only fully capable, but also utterly willing to manufacture evidence, to conceal crucial evidence and even to change the rules that governed life and death if, in the prosecution of the accused, it seemed expedient to do so. Even after all of these years it hurt me to see it. It still hurts me to say it.

As the case lumbered forward under the methodical, minutiae-driven strategy of Ronald Howen, and as our cross-examinations took their toll, it became clear that the FBI had no direct evidence that would tie Randy Weaver physically to the "Y," that now-infamous fork in the faint trail through the trees where Ol' Yella (his real name was Striker), little Sam and Marshal Degan all lost their lives. The truth was virtually undeniable: Randy Weaver had not been at the "Y" at the time of the shooting. When Ol' Yella, barking, took off on the trail after something, Randy had not followed the boys who were hot after Ol' Yella. Instead, he had run in another direction to see if he could cut off the bear or deer everyone thought the dog was trailing. Sometime later Randy heard the shots, and that's when he had called out to Sammy, "Sammy, come home." Kevin Harris told the same story. Randy had not been at the "Y." Later the kids told how their father had arrived home ahead of the others, and how Kevin Harris came plodding back to the house as the agonized bearer of the news that Sammy had been killed. Randy then broke into wild sobbing, rolled on the ground and beat the earth. Finally he grabbed his rifle and shot it into the air, emptied it and loaded it again, time after time, and when he was exhausted it was Vicki, the source of the family's power, and the only person Randy would listen to, who was, at last, able to restrain him.

The marshals had been repeatedly admonished by Washington not to engage the Weavers, and at all costs, not to injure one of the Weaver children. But now they had killed this small boy, shot him in the back. What should they do? At the trial, they claimed they didn't know they had shot the boy, that he must have fallen out of their sight. Yet, as I argued at the trial, they could not have twice shot the child without first seeing him, and, considering his fatal wound through the back, he must have fallen where he was shot. And when later that same day Vicki, Randy and Kevin Harris plodded down to the "Y" to retrieve the body of little Sammy, the marshals, hidden in the trees where they had fired on the dog and the boy in the first place, must have heard their wailing. Had they looked where they shot, they must have seen this weeping mother and this broken father lift up their child, whose wounded arm was dangling by the hide like so much red jerky hung out to dry. And after that they must have seen these three struggle round the bend and disappear out of sight as they headed home bearing their dead.

Rather than go on down and confess to the world what had happened, the marshals stayed huddled in the woods until dark claiming they were surrounded by these crazies, these Weavers. Then under cover of night, the marshals dispatched two of their six to their staging station below to report to the local sheriff that the marshals had been engaged in a horrendous firefight in which they had taken as many as a thousand rounds of fire from the Weavers. They said that Officer Degan had been murdered in the firefight, and that the Weavers were of the Aryan Nations kind, that they were heavily armed, zealous and extremely dangerous and that they had vowed they would never be taken alive. They further added that the marshals were surrounded and required immediate reinforcements. A similar message was dispatched to the marshal's Washington headquarters and thereafter to the FBI. Almost immediately the FBI dispersed its Hostage Rescue Team to Ruby Ridge to save the embattled marshals and to put down these lunatic cultists who had them surrounded.

Not satisfied with this initial report, the marshals the next day supplied an affidavit to the court that blatantly, falsely stated that the Weavers had been shooting at the marshals from a pickup truck. And what about this supposed firefight in which the marshals took as many as a thousand live rounds from the Weavers? During the trial, the most favorable evidence the FBI could provide was that from *both* sides a total of nineteen rounds had been fired—Roderick, the leader of the Marshal's Special Operation Group (SOG) had fired once, the shot that killed Ol' Yella, in response to which Sammy had fired his rifle, a .223, twice. Degan shot seven times. A marshal by the name of Cooper had shot two three-round bursts, six in all. Two shots from the marshal's fire hit and killed Sammy, and in return, Kevin Harris shot three times with his 30–06. If simple arithmetic serves, the marshals fired fourteen rounds while Kevin and Sammy fired five. But the myth of a massive firefight persisted and the myth was obediently recounted by the marshals at trial, because, one would surmise, that if there had been a firefight, well, perhaps it would go a long way in explaining how the marshals came to shoot in the back both a dog and a small boy running home.

Fed by the lip service of the police themselves, the public believes that the police enforce an unwritten code that provides an effective and summary punishment for any who have killed a police officer. People believe that it is far more serious for a citizen to kill a human being who wears a badge than to kill one who does not. The penalty imposed by the police on the cop-killer is, of course, death. During the trial certain facts and circumstances were revealed which, in several camps, argued strongly for the proposition that federal police officers undertook to execute this unwritten rule against the Weavers at Ruby Ridge in retaliation for the death of Marshal Degan. Let me explain.

During the trial the marshals told how in April of 1992, long before the tragic incident at the "Y," the marshals had set up solar-powered microwave video cameras from two positions and at some distance from the Weaver homestead. From these surveillance cameras the marshals had retrieved hundreds of hours of film that provided the marshals' task force with "crucial intelligence information as to what occurs on the compound daily." These videos showed that whenever the Weavers came out of the house, even a trip to the outhouse, they carried their rifles. The cameras showed that when the dogs barked, when vehicles happened by, whenever there were strangers approaching, whenever the Weavers came out to investigate any goings-on, they all carried their rifles, even the kids. But, in the tradition of the Western gun handler, Randy Weaver had taught his family that one never points a gun at another unless one intends to kill that person. Not once did a member of the Weaver family put a gun on any stranger who happened by, or on any marshal or on any other law enforcement officer.

From time to time many people had stopped by the Weaver place, some to seek information about the availability of nearby land, some to ask directions and some just to talk. After cautious inquiry the Weavers proved to be friendly, having even invited some of the folks to come up to the house for cookies. Indeed, more than one of the strangers who happened by, as suspected by the Weavers, were federal marshals looking in on the Weavers as they prepared their strategies to arrest Randy and to bring him down.

The day following the shooting of Marshal Degan (whom the jury later found had been shot by Kevin Harris in self-defense) we see, from the testimony, the Associate Director of the Marshal Service, one Duke Smith, and the leader of the FBI Hostage Rescue Team, one Richard Rogers, being flown from Washington to Ruby Ridge where they would soon take on this "crazy skinhead," Randy Weaver, and his equally "crazy skinhead family." According to the testimony, the two men, their own neatly groomed heads together, are agreeing on a new shoot-on-sight *rule of engagement*. A *rule of engagement* is a euphemism for the authority under which officers are authorized to kill citizens. Under common law, as under the laws of all fifty states, one can intentionally kill another only in self-defense, and then only if one reasonably believes that he or a third person is in imminent peril of death or serious bodily harm. This, too, was the essence of the FBI's traditional *rule of engagement* as set out in its regulations in plain, easy English, a rule by which the FBI and its Hostage Rescue Team were fully bound.

But now we see Rogers changed that rule. As they flew over the broad flat plains toward the mountains of Idaho where Ruby Ridge lay green as rubies are red, the law of the land was changed into a simple order to kill. This new rule was no longer the law of self-defense. Instead, it now read that snipers, bearing their heavy target rifles with their ten-power scopes that can put a bullet into a pea at two hundred yards, could and *should* kill any adult at the Weaver homestead who was armed, whether that person is threatening with a gun or not. Thus, when Randy or Kevin, yes, when even Vicki, innocently walked to the outhouse carrying their rifles, they were dead. Thus, when they ran out to see who had just driven up, as was their well-known habit, and they carried their rifles, which was also their well-known habit, they were dead. The officers who decreed into life this new death-dealing *rule of engagement* must have known from the hundreds of hours of surveillance films the marshals had previously collected that whenever the Weavers left the house they were *always* armed. The result of the new rule was that all the adults at the Weavers would now be shot, thus eliminating the troublesome Weaver problem once and for all, and in effect executing the well-known unwritten penalty imposed by cops against any who kill a cop.

Contemplate the enormity of the power of these two men from separate federal agencies as they changed the law of the land and, according to Eugene Glenn, On Site Commander at Ruby Ridge, and Richard Rogers with the full knowledge and consent of the Assistant Director of the FBI, Larry Potts, in Washington headquarters. They were changing the law by decree, by a bald, secret order, in barely legible handwriting on a small piece of paper, an order that provides that the FBI snipers can and *should* kill any armed male at the so-called "Weaver compound." From the evidence, as we gathered it from our cross-examination, we watched Rogers change the law in the same way that any tyrant rules, by overt edict, one that emerges on the crest of a whim, without the consent, yes, without even the knowledge of the people. Rogers, with the power to command those who are trained to kill and who are willing to kill and who have at their disposal countless instruments of death, thus deployed such men and such instruments under these new death-warrant *rules of engagement.*

It is the rule of law that has, for centuries, protected us from the hoodlum, the gun-happy and the vindictive cop. The rule of law, enacted by a duly elected and convened legislative body, is the mark of the enlightened civilization that distinguishes us from all lower forms of government that have historically enslaved the species. As Smith and Rogers flew a resolute route to Ruby Ridge, the Weavers were unaware that the rule of law had been aborted, and that within hours, the FBI would set up its trap, the fulcrum of which would be this new shoot-on-sight *rule of engage-*

*ment.* Before the day was over, this new rule would account for the killing of Vicki Weaver and the wounding of all of the males still alive at the Weaver homestead.

We were told that before the killing of Vicki Weaver, the *new rule of engagement* had been amended to read that the officers could and should shoot any armed *male,* as distinguished from the original language, any armed *adult,* who presented himself or herself at the Weaver compound. But the claim that there was such an amendment made *before* Vicki was shot is in my opinion suspect, for not only was the original order to shoot any armed *adult*—which, of course, included Vicki—but it was Vicki who, indeed, was thus killed. For it was Vicki who, from the beginning, had been cast by the marshals in the role of the leader, the brains, the heart and soul of the Weaver clan, it having been the marshal's conclusion that none of the Weavers would ever surrender so long as Vicki was alive.

After the shooting and after it became clear that the sniper, Lon Horiuchi, lead man on the FBI Hostage Rescue team, had killed an unarmed mother holding her baby, and considering the fact that no one held a warrant for Vicki's arrest (as the FBI had by then admitted to themselves), it seems more than likely that the *new rule of engagement* was amended, *after* the murder of Vicki Weaver, to provide for the killing of only armed *males.* Without such an amendment, how else could the officers convincingly contend that Vicki Weaver's death had been just a tragic mistake?

But by the time Smith and Rogers arrived at Ruby Ridge, something was obviously amiss. At the scene there was no firefight. That was plain to see. All was silent, except for the heavy rumble of armored military vehicles—tanks of a kind—and the popping propellers of helicopters and the hollering of hundreds of uniformed men setting up their tents and packing their knapsacks, and cleaning their pieces and preparing their equipment for war. And, had they listened into the Weaver yard of large boulders and zinnias blooming like squashed red and yellow balls, they would have heard only the whining of one small dog, who had survived, and the clucking of Rhode Island Red laying hens. And had they listened inside that small flimsy house of plywood scraps, they would have heard the quiet weeping of the mother.

Nevertheless, unbeknown to the Weavers and under the cover of darkness, the FBI spread its Hostage Rescue Team across the way in positions that were unobservable to the Weavers—six skilled sniper sharpshooters with their sniper guns resting readied for the kill along with six observers. The FBI had made no demand that the Weavers surrender before the officers were to fire. Nor had anyone even hinted to the Weavers that six sniper teams waited with their eyes pushed up against their scopes, ready to kill any armed male who walked out the front door.

Then Randy and his sixteen-year-old daughter, Sara, and their friend, Kevin Harris, stepped out, their guns pointed at no one. They were as innocent as small forest animals walking into the jaws of the steel trap. They strolled slowly toward the birthing shed where Randy and Vicki had lain the body of Sammy the day before. Their mission was one of grief, not of hostility. In their injured hearts they suffered the need to see their beloved Sammy one last time before they buried him. To say good-bye. Then, as Randy slowly walked up to the birthing shed and reached up to open the homemade latch, Lon Horiuchi opened fire. Horiuchi's bullet struck Randy through the soft part of his underarm, leaving a neat round hole through and through the size of a lead pencil.

"I'm hit," Randy hollered, and when Sara saw that her father was alive but stunned, she'd jumped in behind him and began pushing him out ahead of her. They had run, the three of them, Kevin in the rear, toward the house. They had run with their backs to the snipers. And, under my cross-examination, Horiuchi admitted that he was trying to kill the running Harris, for was not Horiuchi a sniper trained to kill, committed to kill in accordance with the new *rule of engagement?* And Randy Weaver and Kevin Harris, weren't they armed? More than that, Horiuchi admitted he believed it was Harris, not Weaver, whom he had shot in the first place, although Weaver stands about five feet seven and Harris stands well over six feet tall. And at the door, of course, stood Vicki, armed only with her ten-month-old child, Elisheba, at her breast.

"I'm hit, Momma," Randy had cried to Vicki as he ran toward the door that Vicki had been holding open for them. "I'm hit!"

"Get in here!" Vicki shouted, and those were her last words. We know the rest. Horiuchi's bullet smashed into her head and blew off the side of her face. And after she fell Randy pried the baby from her hands, and Randy and Sara dragged the body of their slain wife and mother over to the side of the kitchen where she lay, her blood flooding the kitchen floor. Sara spread a blanket over her dead mother. And after that, the body lay there for many days in the hot August air, rotting before the sight of the children, before the small child Rachel, the crying baby, and Sara huddled with her father, waiting to be killed. And in the other room, Kevin Harris lay slowly dying of his chest wounds from the same bullet that had killed Vicki, and sometimes he begged Randy to kill him, to take his gun and to shoot him in the head to stop the unbearable agony.

In the meantime, the FBI sent agents who crawled under the house and stuck listening devices under the floor. And although Randy many times screamed out to the officers that they had killed his wife, the officers pretended they did not know she was dead, and they mercilessly taunted the family. "Did you sleep well last night, Vicki?" and "Show us the baby, Vicki?" And, "What did you have for breakfast, Vicki? We had pancakes," and on it went. And the officers placed a robot on the front porch that was equipped with a sawed-off shotgun, and the FBI approached the Weaver house only in an armored personnel carrier, a tank of sorts, and the FBI brought up its negotiator who spoke to the Weavers over a bull horn. The FBI kept spotlights on the small house all night, and played loud music so the people inside could not sleep, and the FBI tried to drive the people, if not out of the house, then out of their minds.

Perhaps by now we have forgotten why Randy Weaver wouldn't come down to be arrested in the first place. He was not a criminal. He had never even collected a speeding ticket during his lifetime. He had been honorably discharged from the Army, collecting a number of meritorious citations. But he had principles, old-fashioned principles, like a belief that a man becomes what he *does*, which, of course, made it quite impossible for him to become a snitch for the Alcohol, Tobacco and Firearms agents.

We still remember that an agent for the ATF, for *our* government, had talked this thoroughly peace-loving man into sawing off a shotgun for money, and, once having talked him into it, the ATF sprung their infamous trap, following which the agents demanded that Randy snitch for them, or else they would charge him with the gun violation and send him to prison. Predictably, Randy told them to go to hell, that he was not going to become a snitch by snitching, a liar by lying, and he was not going to become one who betrays those who trust him by betraying those who trust him. He would not. And it was after that the ATF had set out to arrest him and to bring him down from Ruby Ridge.

The ATF had dawdled around for eighteen months before they finally decided to bring him in. The ATF chose a winter day when Randy and Vicki had set out in their old pickup to fetch some supplies. The marshals' strategy was simple: They parked an old pickup camper on a bridge as if it were stalled. Inside the pickup several heavily armed marshals waited, guns at ready, and another marshal had taken a strategic position above the bridge where he lay in wait in his white camouflage suit, his machine gun leveled on the scene below and at ready. When Randy and Vicki drove up, a man and a woman, both marshals, both dressed in humble country clothes, were peering under the hood. Randy walked up to see if he could help. At that moment the officers emerged from the back of the camper, guns drawn, and put him to the ground. Vicki, too, was thrown to the ground. She later complained she had been immodestly patted down. That night the officers threw Randy in jail and Vicki was released to drive home, alone.

The next day Randy was taken before Magistrate Stephen Ayers who, at the trial, testified that he had released Weaver on his own bond, and under the powerful cross-examination of Chuck Peterson, our associate, the magistrate admitted that he told Weaver that if Weaver appeared for trial and lost, he might lose his house, the family's major asset. That was a fearsome message Randy and Vicki would never forget, and under Peterson's relentless cross-examination, Magistrate Ayers admitted he had misadvised Randy as to the law in this matter. Magistrate Ayers never corrected that error.

Faced with the fear of losing their home if Randy lost his case, Randy and Vicki began to ask simple questions: How could Randy ever win the case? He had sawed off the shotgun, hadn't he? And that was illegal, was it not? And the feds had him cold on audiotape when he sold the sawed-off gun to the undercover ATF agent. Neither Randy nor Vicki were versed in the sophisticated law of entrapment. Nor did they have the advice of any lawyer in this regard. As they saw it, if Randy lost the case, well, then the government would take the family's home, and where would the family go then? And if they were homeless the government would probably take the kids from them as well. As the facts and the law was presented to them they had no alternative but to stay where they were and to pray.

At the hearing, called an "arraignment," the magistrate had set Randy's trial on the gun charge for *February 19*, 1991, but soon thereafter Randy got a letter from the parole and probation officer, who had been assigned to his case, one Karl Richins, a man the magistrate said Randy was to obey. Richins' letter stated in black and white that the trial was set for *March 20*, 1991. And after that, Randy had been shown an article that had appeared in the *Kootenai Valley Times* in which Richins' boss, the head of the department, one Terry Hummell, denied that Richins had ever written such a letter—the letter Randy held right there in his hand. So Randy wondered, how does one believe these government people who lie to you and who lie to the people by lying to the press? How could he submit to any system so evil, he thought. How could he trust these "servants of lawlessness?"

Then he and Vicki and the children had prayed for guidance, and they had received the word, and they sent the word down from Ruby Ridge by letter addressed "To the Servants of the Queen of Babylon" and delivered to the U.S. Attorney, Maurice Ellsworth. The letter, dated March 5, 1991, read as follows:

> "And judgment is turned away backward, and justice standeth afar off; and truth is fallen in the street and equity cannot enter. Yea, truth faileth; and he that departeth from evil is accounted as mad and Yahweh saw it and it displeased Him that there was no judgment." Isayah [sic] 59:14–15.
>
> We the Weaver family, have been shown by our savior and King, Yahshua the Messiah of Saxon Israel, that we are to stay separated on this mountain and not leave. We will obey our lawgiver and King.
> You see the Mighty One of Heaven knows his people. You are servants of lawlessness and you

enforce lawlessness. You are on the side of One World Beastly Government. Repent, for the Kingdom (government) of Yahweh is near at hand.

Chose this day whom you will serve.
As for me and my house—
We will serve Yah-Yahshua, the King.

Whether we live or whether we die we will not obey your lawless government.

(The letter, written in Vicki's perfect script, bore the carefully penned signature of each member of the family who could write, including little Rachel who signed it, very officially, as "Rachel M. Weaver.")

As I revisit the letter just quoted, the word "innocence" seeps to the forefront of the mind, and other words as well, words like "misguided" and "childlike," and "unreasoned," but when I am about to attach such judgments to this naive man, and his prayerful family, I remember that his faith, and the faith of mainstream America are, despite their differences in substance, still faith. Faith is the desperate gift, some say the divine gift, to the man who cannot see God, who understands only his puny, mortal existence—and who is afraid. Afraid, we grasp frantically at whatever protruding twig is within reach as we slip over the canyon wall. Randy Weaver's twig differed from the other twigs to which the masses in America clung, but, at last, they are all twigs and he was as afraid as they, as afraid as we, as afraid as I.

That I find major aspects of their political and religious ideas at extreme odds with my own is not the issue here. Nor do I either apologize or defend Randy and Vicki's beliefs, whatever they were. But when I hear Randy and his family referred to as "cultists," and hated because of that label, hated because they believed differently than most of us, I remember that all believers, whoever they are and whatever they believe, belong to their own cult, and it is only when the cult becomes large enough and powerful enough to dominate major segments of society that the cult loses its label as "cult" and becomes, as if from the beginning, a respectable religion. And so it was with the original Christian cult whose cult members were Christ and the apostles, a cult whose members were required to hide, who held secret meetings under the sign of the fish and who were reviled and hated and finally persecuted and crucified.

The Pilgrims were cultists in England, as were many other sects who found refuge in America. America's heritage is rich in so-called cults, some good, some not, but the right of the citizen to worship as a member of a cult as he or she pleases, has been protected from the beginning under the admonition of the founders that no citizen should be persecuted for his beliefs, for his religion, for his clinging to "cults," no matter how obnoxious, so long as his beliefs do not turn to violence.

As the months passed, David Hunt, the inspector in charge of the local Idaho marshals, had already determined from friendly Weaver sources that the Weavers remained so isolated, so resolute, so armed, because of their fear, based upon Magistrate Ayer's earlier erroneous admonition. Armed with this knowledge, Hunt wrote the Assistant United States Attorney, Ronald Howen, suggesting that simple assurances be given Randy Weaver—that if Weaver surrendered, his home and his children would remain secure. But it didn't take long for Howen to squelch that idea. He responded that the "areas of proposed negotiation are either not within my power to grant or bind the government, too broad in their scope, or are *the type of matters properly addressed in a plea agreement in exchange for guilty pleas, but not mere surrender* [my emphasis]. As I later argued to the jury, and as the Department of Justice investigators thereafter found, Howen had been provided an opportunity early on to seek a peaceful end to this horror, an opportunity he had scornfully dismissed out of hand.

Howen's response argues he was not into a peaceful

solution. I never saw him when he was. His hard-nosed, hardline stance against this frightened little family was, in effect, to say, "Your fear about your home and your kids be damned. You come down and plead guilty, or we will take you the hard way." And with Howen's decision Inspector Hunt had no other choice but to proceed with his plans to capture Randy Weaver.

*During the more than twenty months following the family's* decision not to surrender, the Weavers settled in and prayerfully waited for the prophesied coming of Armageddon. They attacked no one. They threatened no one. Friends brought them their groceries and their mail, which was already being secretly intercepted and examined by the government. Vicki, pregnant with Elisheba, was not able to make her visits to the doctor and had become resolved to deliver the child without the aid of doctor or midwife. During this time the marshal's Special Operations Group (SOG) had established its automatic surveillance cameras and was carrying out its sneak-peek forays in and around the Weaver property preparing to capture this little man who had, by virtue of his audaciousness, become one of the United States Marshal Service's "Major Cases." In response to Randy's elevation to this rare group of murderers, traitors and thugs, the marshals had concocted elaborate plans for Randy's capture, one of which, after the Weavers had been holed up for more than sixteen months, included the kidnapping of Sara.

As the Weavers read the Scriptures, a practice common in early religions and many tribal cultures, the women were to be separated from the rest of the family during their menses. For this purpose the Weaver family had built a special shed which was to serve, as well, as a place where Vicki would endure her labor and deliver her child. The small frame shack was called "the birthing shed." With this in mind the marshals had been charting the dates when Sara was separated to the shed—the same shed in which the corpse of Sammy was later to be lain. This thoroughly outrageous scheme was detailed in writing by the marshals and duly forwarded to Washington for its approval.

The marshals had planned to assemble a task force consisting of five teams including from two to seven marshals each. In addition there would be a command post with one supervisor, two spotters, two riflemen and one backup person. The task force would include two technicians operating the main video below, a command post high up on the mountain, one administrative person, a U.S. Army Medevac team, referred to as "Vulture" (to feast on the carrion?). The Medevac team consisting of two army pilots, one crew chief, and one medic, and there would be a "ruse vehicle" manned by two marshals.

With this force of thirty-three marshals and the other backup personnel, the marshals planned to forcibly take Sara who had committed no crime and for whom the government had no warrant. Indeed, the marshals had been quite observant. Their plan, boldly set out in writing, read, "Based on video surveillance we have determined that Sara begins her menstrual cycle around June 1, 1992. During this time Sara lives in the birthing house as, according to the Weaver beliefs, she is unclean and must remain away from the family until her cycle is over.

"Shortly after all teams are in position at the lower section of the eastern trail, Team 3 would [during the night] move up to the area of the birthing house. The team members would then enter the birthing house, remove Sara Weaver and take her to a secure area. She will be detained and turned over to Boundary County Sheriff, Bruce Whittaker. Team 3 would remain in the birthing house and detain anyone who came out to see Sara . . . By the time the ruse vehicle starts up the road we should have Sara, Sam and Rachel detained and turned over to the county sheriff." After that the ruse vehicle would drive up, and when Weaver came out to investigate, the teams, fulfilling their various assignments, would subdue Weaver.

In the meantime at the trial, Assistant United States Attorney Howen continued his snail's-pace but relentless attack on the supposed beliefs of the Weavers. He called witnesses from the Weavers' hometown in Iowa to testify as to the religious arguments Randy had made. He subpoenaed their old friends to testify about how they sold their house and bought guns and how they had trekked to Idaho, like characters out of *The Grapes of Wrath* in preparation for the coming of Armageddon. Howen subpoenaed one of Randy's skinhead friends to the courtroom, and asked him hostile questions about how Weaver wore his hair, and how the witness and his son wore theirs. And because they were skinheads, it must surely follow that we must hate them, and because we hate them, all of them, Weaver should be convicted of murder.

From the earliest time in the case, Howen sought the death penalty against Randy, surely knowing that no federal law then existing could be stretched to bring about Weaver's execution. And we, Randy's lawyers, were required to petition the court to strike the death penalty request from the case. Sometimes at night I would awaken wondering what would happen if the judge bore the same burning enmity against Weaver as did Howen. What would happen if the judge ignored the law, and the jury convicted Randy? These days one cannot always rely on an appellate court to correct obvious wrongs, for the courts are being smothered with appeals by death-row inmates, and consequently, death penalty cases are often given short shrift. One can be kept sleepless when a single Assistant United States Attorney exercises his power to write those few abominable words on a page, words from which emerge terrible visions of the dangling noose, the dripping executioner's needle, the ready firing squad. One sees them mostly in the night. I never knew what Randy Weaver saw in the night in his small, cold cell, awaiting trial. I never asked him. In a trial, attorney and client most often must fight their own wars, and alone.

If there was a fact to be proven at the trial, Howen proved it, along with every insignificant detail remotely connected to the fact. It was as if in proving a box of corn flakes was indeed corn flakes, he would dump the whole box out on the table and then prove each flake, flake by flake, hour by hour. The trial dragged on. I thought the strategy was to fill the jury with so many facts, to dump on them so much hate, so much fear, so much detail that the jury, from such a mountain of corrupted evidence, would conclude that the prosecution had not only proved its case beyond a reasonable doubt, but that it had proven it ten times over.

But Howen was proving very little, if anything, of substance, and by the time he was required to establish what actually happened at the "Y" where Ol' Yella and little Sammy were killed, the prosecution's case began to crumble. Although Randy was charged with the murder of Degan at the "Y," Randy, as we have seen, was not there when the shots were fired. But what if the FBI produced, say, a certain bullet—a bullet recovered at the "Y" from, say, a gun owned by Randy Weaver, one the FBI had seized at the Weaver house on the day Randy surrendered. What then?

Perhaps the FBI had forgotten that Randy Weaver had been carrying only a twelve-gauge shotgun and a holstered handgun on the day the shooting at the "Y" took place. The bullet that the FBI now produced had been fired from a .223. And how was the bullet found? The FBI claims it found it, a spent bullet, lying daintily on top of some leaves, not buried, not marred or scratched or bent or bruised or dented or otherwise blemished, except, of course, for the rifling that happened to match the .223 rifle that the FBI had seized. But it was not Randy's rifle. It was a rifle belonging to Sara, and Sara had never left the house. Moreover, for the bullet to travel from the house to the "Y," it would have had to magically travel straight through more than a half a mile of dense timber without touching, not once, a tree or a twig, and it would have had to land perfectly on top of the leaves, land in such a way as to appear it had been carefully laid there, which is not the known dynamic of bullets as they spend themselves.

Think of it! Another magic bullet, like in the Oswald case? We remembered that bullet, of course, the one the FBI seemingly produced out of nowhere during the assassination investigation. It had supposedly passed though flesh and bone and bone and flesh of both President Kennedy and Governor Connally, and having done so, it was conveniently found right there in the gurney, pristine and pretty and as utterly unmarked as the day it had been manufactured.

In Randy's trial, we challenged not only the bullet itself, but the means by which it had gotten to the "Y". Under my cross-examination, the FBI agent who recovered the bullet admitted that he had manufactured evidence that was to later illustrate its discovery. The agent claimed he found the bullet, picked it up and put it in his pocket. Then he claimed he later thought that he should take a photo of it to record how and where the bullet lay when he supposedly found it. So the agent took the bullet back to the place where he thought he found it, took it out of his pocket again, placed it on the ground and took a picture of it. One would wonder if he could even remember in what direction the bullet had been pointing. The photo, of course, was posed. But it had not been offered as a posed picture. Government officers, our servants, ought not to attempt to put citizens in prison for life based on posed pictures of magic bullets. I thought once more of old Andy Sutka.

And, of course, we remember that Lon Horiuchi, who had taken the stand, had testified that, indeed, he had intended to kill Kevin Harris, who was running for his life, his back to the sniper. Yet the prosecution claimed that the sniper, who admittedly could see and hit a fly at two hundred yards with his ten-power scope, could not see the head of Vicki Weaver through the glass window of the open door. Instead, the prosecution attempted to make the jury believe that the curtains were closed. But from my own discussion with Randy that fact seemed in question, especially after the government failed to produce a crucial Horiuchi drawing of what the sniper had seen when he fired.

From the drawing made by Horiuchi during an interview with the FBI at a hotel, on hotel stationery, he draws in no closed curtains at all. In the lower right-hand corner of the window we see two partial heads as if people were squatting there. Indeed, Randy and Sara had dived into the house just ahead of Kevin Harris. And it was Harris, not Weaver, who presumably had killed a federal officer, and who Horiuchi himself was admittedly trying to kill, whether or not he was carrying out the unwritten law that seemed to doom the cop-killer. Be that as it may, the method of hitting a running target is for the shooter to place the "mildot" seen in the scope on the target—Harris in this case—which places the crosshairs ahead of the target, thus leading the target, so the bullet and the target will arrive simultaneously. Shortly after the killing this is exactly as Horiuchi himself drew it for the FBI interrogator.

Horiuchi's drawing shows us that he must have known that human beings were behind the flimsy door. He had to know that someone, presumably Vicki or the ten-year old Rachel, was likely standing behind the door to hold it open. Moreover, the drawing proves he knew exactly where in the door he planned his bullet to strike. And that's where it did strike—at the cross, as he shows it in the drawing. Vicki Weaver's head was behind the cross, that apocalyptic symbol, which served also as the point of aim for the killer.

When Howen confessed to the judge that the FBI had withheld this pivotal piece of evidence, Horiuchi's drawing, His Honor, Edward Lodge, was irate. A legal as well as a moral obligation demands that the government produce all of its exculpatory evidence in its possession, that is, all evidence that is favorable to the defendant. From the outset we had told the jury that the evidence would establish that Mrs. Weaver was intentionally shot by the federal agent. The Horiuchi exhibit, withheld from us by the FBI, supported the conclusion that, at a minimum, the sniper knew human beings were behind the door into which he was shooting, presumably Vicki. But perhaps the drawing, along with the killing of Vicki Weaver, implied more—that Horiuchi could see where his bullet would strike, that with his high-powered scope he could plainly make out the most minute details of Vicki Weaver's head and frightened face.

What does a judge do with an omnipotent FBI that will violate the law as well as the rights of innocent citizens by withholding evidence that is crucial to freedom? I suspect that Judge Lodge believed this grave wrong was not the creation of a single person, but was the product of a conspiracy, of sorts, among several. If it was likely impossible for the judge to determine who, exactly, was responsible for withholding this evidence, well, he could hardly put the Bureau itself in jail, nor would the Bureau fit into any public stocks to there be flogged as was the punishment for miscreants in colonial days. And so the judge, attempting to do at least something, admittedly, not very much, sanctioned the Bureau for its misconduct by requiring it, the Bureau, to pay the defense attorneys one day's fees. I wondered whose budget in the Bureau this piddling sum would come from—petty cash, the stamp fund, the party fund, if any? Since Kent, my son and I as well as Gary Gilman were representing Randy without fee, and since we wanted to accept nothing from the government for Randy's defense, not even sanction money, we made no effort to collect it, and, predictably the United States has made no effort to pay it. Nothing but a pretty fantasy supposes that a few thousand dollars in sanction money, which no agent must personally pay, will in the future deter the FBI from hiding critical evidence. Yet the court's order was a public slap in the face to the Bureau. A respected United States District Judge had officially found that the FBI will cheat to win a case. Once more I thought of old Andy Sutka.

The judge and the jury freed Randy Weaver of all charges, except for his failure to *appear* for his trial on the gun case. He was in jail for a month or so after the trial, but Judge Lodge gave him credit for the months he had remained in jail awaiting trial and for the nearly three months that the trial itself had taken. He was released before Christmas of 1993 when he returned to the place of his childhood, the long bleak winter farm country of Iowa.

*With Vicki dead, Randy stayed at home to attend to the moth-*ering of toddling Elisheba. Sometimes he lamented the fact that he fell short as a mother. He was and is a shy man. He usually does not want to talk to the press. He does not wish to be a symbol or a hero for any of the far right radical fringes with whom, he says, he would likely disagree. He lives on the meager pittance he receives from Social Security paid as a result of Vicki's death. He has not sold his rights to movies or books or to tabloid television. He wishes the death of his beautiful wife and his loving son to stand for something. And he grieves, and he is lonely and he struggles to forget, but he remembers that he is an American citizen, and that the rule of law was supposed to protect him and his family, and he tries to understand how, in America, the servants of the people became "the servants of the lawless," how federal officers who are charged with keeping the people safe, should become the killers of women and children, the innocent, whom the federal police are charged to protect. He wonders how, at last, these servants should become the people's fearful oppressors.

Still, Randy Weaver ponders in the night, as even have I. What lessons, what wisdom, what meaning we may glean from this horror that Randy Weaver and his children have endured at the hands of their own government?

Before the trial, and presumably to aid the prosecution at the trial, the FBI did a quick and dirty internal investigation that whitewashed the whole Randy Weaver affair. Nobody did anything wrong. The officers' acts, including the murders, were all sweet roses and tulips. But after the trial, at our urging and the urging of others, the Department of Justice assembled an investigative team consisting of a number of their top agents from around the country, as well as lawyers from the Department of Justice itself. The report of this team took over a year to assemble, and is a massive document of five hundred forty-two pages. It purports to discover what went wrong in the Randy Weaver case. It finds, among other things, that the FBI's "roses and tulips report" was inadequate and negligently done, and the agents responsible for this whitewash were either censured or reprimanded. One was suspended fifteen days. Two others were given letters of reprimand or censure but reportedly had already retired.

As for Ronald Howen, he was referred to the Executive Office for the United States Attorneys, the disciplinary arm of the United States Department of Justice, "for whatever action it deems appropriate." Howen was criticized for, among other things, "significant defects in the indictment" and for the lack of a proper review process that "would insure more relevant charges." The Deputy Attorney General's memorandum to Louis Freeh, the Director of the FBI, charged that Howen should not have rejected the marshal's plan to negotiate surrender terms with Weaver. That deficiency, and others, "forced the Marshal's Service to engage in extraordinary efforts to plan and execute a non-confrontational alternative to require Weaver to respond to the warrant. It was on the reconnaissance phase of this extraordinary plan that the confrontation occurred." The Justice Department further found that the U.S. Attorney's office "drafted an inappropriately broad and aggressive indictment"—in plain words, they should not have thrown in the kitchen sink and asked for the death penalty—and failed to provide for internal review thereof and that the U.S. Attorney's office engaged in misconduct before the grand jury (probably a reference to the explicit hearsay testimony concerning the supposed horrendous crimes of the Order which were totally unconnected to Randy Weaver.) But this should not have been any news to the Department of Justice, for in December, before the trial began, we had already filed a fully documented motion to disqualify Howen for misconduct, and we had petitioned the Department of Justice to appoint a special prosecutor, all of which was declined both by the court and the department. It was only after Randy Weaver had walked through and endured the painful coals of the trial that the Department of Justice, in effect, made many of the same findings after the trial that we had complained of before the trial had begun.

I am told that Howen, at this writing, is no longer

prosecuting criminal cases and, instead, is employed by the civil division of the United States Attorney's Office. No disciplinary action has been taken against him as far as we know.

The Justice Department further found that the assumptions of the federal officers concerning Weaver—"that he was a former green beret, that he would shoot on sight anyone who attempted to arrest him, that he had collected certain types of arms, that he had 'booby-trapped' and tunneled his property [which was utterly false but which was alluded to during the trial] exaggerated the threat he posed."

Eugene F. Glenn, the "On-Site Commander at Ruby Ridge," was censured for his "inadequate performance as On-Site Commander" in approving the *new rules of engagement*, and for his failure to adequately and personally address the poor working relationship with the United States Attorney's office. He received a fifteen-day suspension and was removed from his field command. The FBI claims Richard Rogers voluntarily left the Hostage Rescue Team. He was assigned to fieldwork. He was also suspended for ten days. The Department of Justice, despite the killings of two innocent people, a mother and son, did not choose to prosecute *anyone.* Yet this same government was only too eager to prosecute two of its citizens who had committed no legal wrongs at all, and was willing to manufacture and secrete evidence to accomplish the same.

At this writing Glenn claims that Larry Potts, then the Assistant Director of the FBI at FBI Headquarters in Washington, D.C. was fully aware of the new shoot-on-sight rule of engagement adopted for Ruby Ridge, and that Potts signed off on it, a claim which Potts now denies. Glenn identifies two other witnesses high up in the FBI who support his assertion. The FBI agent in charge of this internal investigation, one Charles Matthews, III, found that, "the rules of engagement are considered unconstitutional; therefore, there is no need to further discuss them." Potts was censured for failure to clearly define the rules of engagement, and then promptly *promoted* to Deputy Director of the FBI, the clear message to all in government and elsewhere being that if an agent of the FBI aborts the law by decree and such unconstitutional act results in the killing of innocent people, especially if the people harbor beliefs different from our own, those responsible persons at headquarters will be promoted, and those in the field who carry out the killings will only be censured and given a few days vacation without pay.

Lon Horiuchi, the trigger man, received neither suspension nor censure.

Then came the cowardly bombing at Oklahoma City. The world has indeed changed. But as the world changes, our fervent love of freedom *must* not change. The federal police are not composed of the Andy Sutkas of the country. Perhaps none of the police ever were. The friendly quiet villages of my childhood, where people lived without fear and loved their neighbors and left their keys in their cars and their doors unlocked at night have mostly disappeared. The earth has become a dangerous place in which to live. But we must not surrender our simple faith in freedom, for freedom has always been risky, and its price has always been high.

Still, Lord Acton's sage rejoinder endures: "Power tends to corrupt, and absolute power corrupts absolutely." When we face the heinous and dastardly tragedy of the Oklahoma City bombing, one of our first concerns becomes *our* protection. "Protect us," we beseech the government. "Protect us, the people, from our enemies, from the fringes and the radicals and the crazies. Protect us from those who bear arms, from those who believe differently than we, from those we fear, whether we fear with justification or not. Protect us from our neighbors, from aliens, from terrorists, protect us from everyone, including ourselves."

And the government, the embodiment of power that yearns always for more power, responds, "Give the government more of your freedom. Freedom is the price you must pay for your safety. Let us tap your phones more easily. Let us break into your homes without warrants. Let us snoop and spy on you and your families and your neighbors. Let us have more police. Give the government more power." And out of the ethos, if one were to listen, one might hear the high sweet voices of Vicki and little Sammy whispering, "Listen once more to our story. Power is a dreadful disease. We were the victims of power. We were murdered by power. Give the government more agents? More agents to entrap you and to frighten you, to oppress you and to tell all measure of untruths against you, and, at last, more agents to murder you and to prosecute your family for crimes they did not commit?"

Or, perhaps, if you listen, you will hear nothing.

But have we not already identified the enemy of freedom? The enemies of freedom are not the fringes and the radicals and the crazies or those who want to own guns. *We* are the enemy. Our *fear* is the enemy—our fear that would allow a couple of lunatic bombers at Oklahoma City to corner two hundred and fifty million of us with fear, in response to which and in exchange for the bald promise of protection, we are petitioned by the government to abdicate our freedom and renounce our sacred rights as free people.

The lesson of the Weaver trial must never become the vindication of Weaver's beliefs, but, instead, the need of all Americans freely to believe as they will, without risk of persecution by a government or by a majority or by a power clique. And to preserve this precious birthright we must dedicate our constant attention, our unmitigated courage and our purest full energy.

The enemy is, indeed, our fear of mad dogs like those who struck at Oklahoma City. Yet there have always been mad dogs in our society who will attack the innocent flock. But will there not also always be the willing, waiting wolf, the hungry wolf standing by who will offer to protect us from the mad dogs, if only we will deliver ourselves to the wolf?

Eternal vigilance is still the price of freedom, eternal vigilance, and today, more than ever, courage. For now, as always, it takes courage to remain free.

# 3

# EASY IN THE HARNESS

## *The*

## *Tyranny*

## *of*

## *Freedom*

*"What is freedom?" an enlightened teacher asked her class.*

"It's when you can leave home and go wherever you want, and do whatever you want, and your parents can't tell you what to do," a child replied.

"But what if you get hungry? Are you now free to starve?"

"I would go home," the child says.

We are not free. Nor have we ever been. Perfect freedom demands a perfect vision of reality, one too painful for the healthy to endure. It requires that we be alive, alert, and exquisitely aware of our raw being. Faced with the pain of freedom, man begs for his shackles. Afraid of death, he seeks the stultifying boundaries of religion. Afraid of loneliness, he imprisons himself in relationships. Afraid of want, he accepts the bondage of employment. Afraid of rejection, he conforms to the commands of society. If our knowledge of freedom were perfect we would not choose it. Pure freedom is pure terror.

Freedom is like a blank, white canvas when no commitments, no relationships, no plans, no values, no moral restraints have been painted on the free soul. A state of perfect freedom is a state of nothingness. When we care for another, when we make room for another's wants and needs, we have lost an equal portion of our freedom, but in the bargain we are freed of loneliness. When we take on marriage and a family, we are bound by our vows, the law, and our moral commitments to spouse and child, but our bargain frees us of detachment and meaninglessness. When we live in the country we can drive our trucks across the prairies, but when we join a community we cannot drive our cars across our neighbors' lawns. We can abide by no moral values without being limited by them. We can belong to no clubs without agreeing to their rules, or to a neighborhood without recognizing the rights of our neighbors. When we become residents of a village, a state, or a nation, we must obey its laws. In short, when we join into any relationship our dues are always paid in freedom.

Robert Frost understood freedom and expressed its essence in a typical Frostian metaphor: "Freedom is when you are easy in the harness." Easy in the harness. I used to sit behind a team of good horses, Star and Spiffy, and together we mowed the meadow hay. Their flanks foamed with sweat and after struggling for weeks at their tugs, sores developed on their necks from their rubbing collars. I remember a deep, sad look in the eyes of the horses. I liked to touch the horses, to feel their softer-than-velvet noses against my cheek. I liked their smell. I loved old Star and Spiffy.

I suppose that team of horses was mostly "easy in the harness." Willingly they would trudge up and down the field all day, their heads down, their tugs tight, their flanks digging like the pistons of engines, and at the end of the day when I lifted the wet harnesses from their backs they would run for the corral and lie down in the deep dust and roll, and roll again. Then they would get up and shake the dust from their backs and wait for me to open the corral gate to the pasture.

One spring when I returned to the ranch I found Star and Spiffy gone. Nobody wanted to talk about it. "They're just gone," the old rancher said.

"But where?" I asked.

"Gone," was all he would say, and the way he said it with such finality made it clear that was to be the end of it. Later I learned that each fall a horse buyer visited the neighboring ranches to buy the ranchers' worn-out nags. They brought a few cents a pound for dog meat. Some claimed the meat was shipped to Europe where horse meat was allegedly a delicacy, especially with the French, but I never confirmed it.

As I look back on it the horses were as easy in their harnesses as we. And their deaths were perhaps better than our own. I could see in my mind's eye the old team being shipped off, the eyes of the old horses as sad as ever. But it was only another ride to them. They were not being trucked to their execution. Their bellies were not gripped with fear. There was no sadness, no regrets. And as the truck rumbled down the highway toward the slaughterhouse, the fall air must have blown through their manes and made their old tired eyes water, and they must have felt joy.

Every day we spend our freedom like careless children with too many pennies. In exchange for acceptance by our friends we give up the right to say what we think. Being socially proper is more important than possessing a fresh, uncompromised soul. Being acceptable to our neighbors is often more important than being acceptable to ourselves. For nearly two hundred years slavery thrived in America over the silent protestations of decent citizens enslaved themselves by the tyranny of convention. The price of freedom is often rejection, even banishment.

I knew an old rancher who lived on the Wind River in Wyoming. People didn't have much good to say about old Jack. His chief crime was that he told the truth as he saw it and laughed at things we were all afraid to laugh at. Every once in a while I'd stop by to see him. He was usually in his garden. That day he was hoeing his corn, a special hybrid variety he had developed for our short growing season, and he was also locally famous for his high-altitude peas and potatoes.

"Well, what has God wrought today?" I asked, knowing full well my question would engender a strong response.

"You talkin' 'bout *me*," he replied. "I'm my own god."

"Jack, aren't you afraid of going to hell for saying such irreligious things?"

"There ain't no hell 'cept on earth." He went on hoeing. His shirt was wet with good fresh summer sweat.

"Suppose God heard you say that," I said prodding him a little. "What if he condemned you to burn in hell for an eternity for such heresy?" I'd been introduced to such horrors as a child in Sunday school.

"No just god would condemn ya fer usin' the power of reason he give ya," he said, "and the idea of hell is plumb unreasonable." He stopped, leaned on his hoe handle, and squinted at me. "Besides, who would want ta worship a god that would send yer ass to hell forever fer such a triflin' transgression as not believin' somethin' that is unreasonable? That would be no *just* god, and if he ain't just I don't want nothin' ta do with him."

The old boy was already well past eighty and he knew that by all odds his days were numbered. "How you been feeling, Jack?" I asked, trying to change the subject.

"Feel just perty perfect," he said. Then he went back to hoeing. "But I may not make it another winter."

The following spring I stopped by. He was on his hands and knees planting his garden.

"Well, Jack, I see you made it through another winter."

"Yep," he said. "See ya done the same."

"God willing," I said.

"God didn't have nothin' ta do with it," he said.

"How come you're so tough on God?" I asked.

"On accounta those kinda ideas hurt a lotta innocent folks," he said. He never looked up from his planting while he talked. He dropped the brown bean seeds about an inch apart in the shallow furrow. "Christ taught that love is the supreme law. But they got it all mixed up. I got a lotta neighbors that love God and hate each other. I say if yer gonna love, ya oughta love something ya can see, say, yer neighbor fer instance."

He had radical ideas for his time, for instance his views on birth control, about which he spoke often and freely. "This here earth is overrun with people. The multitudes is starving everywhere. Now when I can't feed no more cows on this little ranch I sure don't raise no more calves. There ain't no starvin' calves here," he said. He covered the seed with his old crooked fingers and tamped the fresh, moist soil over them with the heels of his hands. "So how come my cows has got better rights than people? What kind of a god would want ya to raise up kids ta starve?

When he got to the end of the row he stood up, stretched his old stiff back, and looked at me for the first time. "Why them churchgoin' neighbors a mine claim to love the fetus in the womb. But as soon as the kid is born, they say it's all right if it's left ta starve. I never could figure out why little kids who never done nothin' ta nobody should be punished by bein' sentenced ta starve ta death fer no worse crime than being born in the first place." When he looked at me I never saw a kinder set of eyes. I never knew a more honest man. I never knew a man who was more free than old Jack. But I think Jack was lonely sometimes. And, to the wonder and secret disappointment of some of his neighbors who were put off by his harsh and unedited comments on religion, and who thought for sure he'd never make it another winter, he lived through a dozen more after that.

Sometimes when I think of old Jack I realize how unfree I am, how afraid, how timid and intimidated and how the bargains I make sometimes leave me feeling cheated, how I sometimes trade honest convictions for silence to gain acceptance by those around me. Yet, in the end, I doubt that my neighbors love me any more than Jack's loved him. They respected him, that much I know, and maybe Jack valued their respect more than their love. Yet respect and love are sometimes hard to separate.

Jack's neighbors all came to his funeral, and some who had been his most severe critics had tears in their eyes. I doubt that Jack would have been surprised. I think he knew.

They buried old Jack out behind his garden where he wanted, close to the creek. As they lowered the pine box into the ground I could hear his creaky old voice arguing away. "Why, Spence," he said, "we kick our dogs if they shit in the house, but we shit all over this beautiful planet like a herd a hogs sufferin' from terminal diarrhea. Baby owls are smarter'n that. Ya never seen a baby owl that ever fouled its nest. These human bein's ain't too smart a species."

And I thought, Well, Jack, your old bones won't pollute this little plot behind your garden, that's for sure. Next spring you'll turn into fresh buds on the cottonwood trees, and maybe you won't think that's too bad a place to be. Maybe that's eternity after all. Earth to earth.

"Beats hell outta hell," I could hear old Jack reply. And then I turned away before the neighbors could catch up with me to tell me all about how old Jack was. One thing I knew: Old Jack was free. Always had been.

\* \* \*

*The notion of "being American" is heavily laden with ideas* of freedom. Being American and being free are often thought synonymous. As Americans we envision Washington's battered patriots marching to the beat of the boy drummer. We see Washington crossing the Delaware. We think of the Constitution and the Bill of Rights, and remember the Civil War, Lincoln and the Gettysburg Address, the freeing of the slaves, the great world wars "to keep America free." We see the billowing smoke of the ships sinking at Pearl Harbor and our American heroes raising the flag at Iwo Jima. And we remember the marches of Martin Luther King, Jr. We believe we are free in the same way we believe in God. Freedom is an article of faith, not a fact, not a condition. True, the freedom we enjoy in America, when set against the freedom of peoples in other lands, is emblazoned like a single candle lighting the gloom.

Law and order and rules, although antithetical to freedom, provide us with safeguards by which we are free to live with reasonable safety among those who are stronger. But the strong impose themselves upon us nevertheless. Although our younger, stronger neighbor is not free to force us out of our homes, the bank can do so if we fail to pay it its tribute of green flesh. Although we argue we are free to labor where we please for whomever we please, unless we show up in the morning, unless like old Star and Spiffy, we take our places in our stanchions and consent to the harness, we will be free to join the depressed and desperate masses of the unemployed who become harnessed to yet another master—fear.

If we are American, we believe in an American religion called "free enterprise," the principal tenet of which holds that it is not only moral but divine to reserve for the corporate oligarchy substantially all the wealth—leaving to the people the blessed right to obtain whatever, if any, dribbles down. The religion called "free enterprise" holds that in exchange for corporate America's right to squash and squeeze from all

57

below it, the next in power possess the right to squash and squeeze those below them, and so on down the line until there is nothing left but the empty dredges of humanity. Some of these we discard on the streets, where they are free to die of hunger, disease, and shame. Those who rebel are at last housed—in prisons.

I think of a poem attributed to a fictional character I once created, a poet I called George Henry Short who claimed Jimmy Carter had nearly appointed him as America's Poet Laureate. The poem was so powerful, George Henry claimed, that it catapulted him out of contention for the honor. The poem, laconically entitled "We Should Cut Ronnie's Throat and Let the Bastard Bleed to Death in the Blue Room of the White House, But in My Heart I Know He Loves Me," was as follows:

> *On Tuesday afternoon I sat on a park bench*
> *Across from the White House,*
> *Across from Rathole Jenkins, a street person*
> *Who was, at said time and place,*
> *Occupying the green bench*
> *Under the third sycamore tree*
> *Next to a garbage can.*
>
> *Rathole Jenkins had a*
> *Program called "The Clearances."*
> *"Clear out all the poor," he hollered from a*
> *Prone position underneath yesterday's newspaper*
> *With headlines that read:*
> *"Fourteen Million Homeless Clog the Machinery."*
> *"Clear out the bag ladies.*
> *Clear out all the cripples in*
> *Their chrome-wheeled wheelchairs*
> *And the wackos in the a-sylums.*
> *(Rathole Jenkins always said "a-sylums.")*
> *Zap 'em! I say.*
> *Zap 'em 'til their eyeballs pop out*
> *And they slobber tapioca pudding.*

*Clear out that crazy blind nigger bum*
*From under the bridge.*
*All he does is cry and look into the sun.*
*Clear out that limpin' dog-faced hag*
*Who sleeps on the Constitution Avenue grates*
*With her baby daughter*
*Who runs around bawlin' all day*
*With a snotty nose*
*And without diapers,*
*For Kee-rist sakes!*

*"Clear out all the dregs of modern capitalism.*
*We don't need 'em any more*
*Than we need coffee grounds.*
*I say, Clear out our leavin's."*

*Now Rathole Jenkins got up*
*And started rummaging*
*Through the garbage can.*
*"America ain't designed ta be the home a the poor.*
*She ain't no storehouse fer bums*
*Or old fogies with sticky gums*
*Who refuse to use*
*Polident*
*(I personally have no use for them*
*Who refuse to use Polident.)*
*America is the home of the brave*
*And the beautiful*
*Who wear pants by Docker's, by God."*

*Then Rathole Jenkins*
*Concluded his argument:*
*"And if Reagan don't want to go along with this*
*Wholly reasonable program,*
*Well, then I say we should cut Ronnie's throat*
*and let the bastard*
*Bleed to death*
*In the Blue Room of the White House.*
*But in my heart I will always know he loves me."*

Yet as Rathole Jenkins might have admitted, had we inquired, none are more free than the homeless, none possess more liberty than the "leavings" of the system.

Today we are more concerned with extracting freedom from our enemies than in preserving our own. We wish into prison those who terrorize us in the streets and who break into our cars and homes. We wish the executioner's hand against those who kill our innocent without just cause. At last we wish to eliminate all those from our society who threaten us and frighten us and injure and kill us, and we seem willing to diminish or release our constitutional rights, indeed, our freedom, to be safer. In truth, we long for a more successful domestication of the human species.

I recall a certain white heifer at the ranch, a full-blown renegade. When she was disturbed in the slightest she would run bellowing and bawling and wildly kicking at everything and anything, including the air. To get her from one pasture to another took half a dozen good men on good horses half a day. I would have sent her to the butcher but for the fact that I had paid a pretty price for her one crazy afternoon at a fancy purebred sale that had been held in the lobby of the Hilton Hotel in Denver.

When her calf came, the calf was just like her. The little renegade wasn't more than a few days old when it kicked the old dog and broke his jaw. But for the fact that the calf in all other respects was quite a beautiful specimen and would bring a good price, I would have rid the ranch of her as well. But the calf's calf was even worse. Finally I realized I was breeding back to the wildebeest, and that unless I abandoned that bloodline, I would end up with an utterly unmanageable herd of cattle that would eventually do me in.

Domestication has been the specialty of man from the beginning. He domesticated the wolf into the dog, the wildcat into the lap pussy, the wild horse into the plow horse, the wildebeest into the Hereford and the Holstein. He has also been busily domesticating himself. As in the domestication of animals he has been selecting the most compliant members of his species and eliminating the least.

Today, America imprisons more people than any nation in the world. Those who occupy our prisons have been our noncomplying social deviants, whom we have removed from the reproductive cycle. In recent times we have become more willing to impose the death penalty against our own for a broader assortment of crimes. Facing proof that the death penalty has no deterring effect on crime whatsoever, we nevertheless encourage its imposition out of our true purpose, not to punish, not to prevent future crimes, but to further domesticate the species by eliminating those who are less compliant than we.

Something about servitude stills. Something about domestication stifles. The wolf, now the poodle, no longer howls. The wild boar lies on its side in the hog pen and grunts. The wildebeest stands in her stall placidly chewing her cud while she's milked dry. Domestication of man and beast muffles the cry of freedom and suffocates the spirit of liberty.

As we continue to domesticate the species, we tend toward the creation of a mass of mankind that is as easily herded as a flock of dead-eyed sheep. This amorphous glob faithfully mumbles the liturgy demanded by the corporate oligarchy, which holds that it is moral to take first and most from the weakest and the poorest. The dogma also holds that it is laudable to create classes of people based on wealth, not virtue, that is to say, it makes no difference how miserly, how greedy, how uncaring and spiteful the individual may be, if he has wealth he is of a different and better class than the virtuous without wealth. This religion to which the people are bound delivers to the corporate oligarchy the prerogative to ply its enormous powers against the people in order to become yet more powerful. And so it has been throughout human history as man struggles for his freedom, fights and dies for it, but having once achieved it, squanders it or casts it aside as too naked, too frightening, too painful to long possess.

I think of the wars that have been fought, allegedly for freedom. More often the blood and suffering and death were sacrificed so that massively powerful mon-eyed interests might remain free to use us up in our harnesses. I think of the endless list of the dead who were said to have given their lives so that we might be free. But after the wars nothing much changed. As usual we arose every morning, slipped into our har-nesses, plodded to our work, and believed we were free. Then we died.

We all wear our harnesses, and if we are easy in them, if we feel free, is not the illusion of freedom as satisfactory as freedom itself? Should we fret over our servitudes, petty or grand, when the fictions of freedom we embrace often serve as satisfactorily? Is not a shack-led slave who cannot see or feel his chains as free as if he had no chains at all? Should we free the happy slave and cast him into the chaos and horrors of pure free-dom? Indeed, have we not at last achieved the predic-tion of *Brave New World,* in which Aldous Huxley observed that the "really efficient totalitarian state would be one in which the all-powerful executive of political bosses and their army of managers control a population of slaves who do not have to be coerced, because they love their servitude"? Huxley argued that, "To make them love it [their bondage] is the task as-signed, in present-day totalitarian states. . . . " Ought we not consider the possibility that the *1984* of George Orwell has come and gone and that his once chilling oracle is the culture of our time, one in which we do, in fact, love our bondage, one where, in fact, we hap-pily accept the clichés, the images, the fables, and the fictions of freedom in the place of freedom itself?

Freedom, "that sweet bondage," as Shelley called it, is a marvelous thing in small doses. Not to be afraid of our government is blessed. Not to be lied to, not to be cheated, not to be exploited and poisoned and hurt for corporate greed, not to be used up like old rags; to be heard, to be respected, to grow and to discover our uniqueness—these are the freedoms we most cherish, freedoms we, by reason of our occupancy of this earth, are entitled to enjoy.

Yet most of our freedoms lie within. As the poem goes, "Stone walls do not a prison make, nor iron bars a cage." Most freedoms cannot be given, except as we give them to ourselves.

I think of old Jack who cherished his freedom above all. He is, at last, free, totally free, since freedom, by common definition, is a condition in which the individual may do what he wants, and since the dead have no wants they are, are they not, totally free? Or perhaps as the Greeks argued, "Only Zeus is free."

And I also think of old Star and Spiffy, and of their freedom. Were I as successful, as free. Were I able to mow the meadows of my life and live by my own work as well. Were I able to remove the harness from within—such is freedom. And when finally the legs have given out, when the bones are old and brittle and crooked, and at last the shoulders too crippled to pull the load, I should hope that on the way to wherever it is that old horses and old men go I feel the wind through my hair, and that my eyes do not water from tears, but from having felt the joy of the trip, the trip to the last and only freedom.

# T H E  I N V I S I B L E  T R A P

*The*

*Tyranny*

*of*

*Fear*

*The sides of the grave are lined with blankets of that stiff* artificial green, green grass undertakers use to hide the sight of hard earth, of grass roots and tree roots chopped through by the gravedigger's shovel. The green grass blankets distract the mourners from the cold fact that the body will be lowered into six feet of dirt and gravel, that it would be buried—buried and at last forgotten.

Inside the coffin the smell of the undertaker's cheap perfume covers the ascerbic odor of formaldehyde. Although the corpse does not breathe, although its heart is still and stiff, the blood coagulated in its veins, the arteries collapsed and sunken, although the long, stainless-steel trocar has been inserted into the stomach and the contents sucked out and replaced with chemicals, still the corpse does not know that it is dead.

At the funeral parlor the corpse had put on quite a show. Shortly after the organist had begun playing

"The Requiem," the corpse it suddenly rose up from the satin and opened its eyes. What it saw cannot be known, for the corneas were wrinkled and the eyes dull and empty. Although the jaws had been wired shut so as not to permit the mouth to sag open, the corpse then began to emit long, flat sobs through its clenched teeth.

"Do not shut the lid," the corpse cried. "I do not want to die."

"But you are already dead," the attendant replied politely.

"How can I be dead?" the corpse cried back. "I have never lived."

"Of course you have lived. And your time has come. Now be nice. Don't cause trouble. Let us shut the lid."

Then the corpse began to ululate—an endless, breathless wail as if a thief had entered its body and the alarm had sounded. And to stop the horrid noise, the attendants rushed up and slammed down the lid. Even then, the muffled screams escaped through the pores of the coffin. The lead attendant turned to the mourners and smiled a sad but reassuring smile.

"Don't be concerned," he said. "We often encounter deceaseds who are unwilling to accept the fact that they are dead. It happens all the time. We apologize for the disturbance. But once we get them buried, it will be all right. In fact, that is why the dead are buried." He gave another tiny, mirthless smile and then quickly joined the attendants, who lost no time in rolling the coffin out of the room and into the waiting hearse.

More chilling is the scene we observe every day—the *breathing* dead who believe they are alive. Year after year these breathing dead get up at the same time every morning on the same side of bed, trudge to the same kitchen, swallow the same brand of bacon and style of eggs for breakfast, drive the same route to work, and wearily enter the same door of employment where automatically they punch the same time clock and perform, like machines, the same mindless task until the same bell goes off at five o'clock. Then by rote they return home in order to open the same brand of beer, and to watch the news on television that informs them of the same murders and violence, which are balanced against the same insipid sitcoms evoking the same canned laughter. Ha. Ha.

The breathing dead emulate machines. Their work is mechanical. They relate more to the simulated life on television than to their own species. It's safer to love the electronic image, safer to engage a nonbeing. Moreover, the control of their television sets provides a power they do not possess in life, the power of the thumb that clicks from electronic life to electronic life and the power to extinguish such life at will. The bargain seems fair. By relinquishing their own lives, which can be petty, puny, and powerless, they acquire a nonlife over which they can exercise complete and final power.

I would rather visit with the corpse than exist with the breathing dead, with those who have never considered a new idea, who worship the same God and vote the same party of their fathers, whose friends believe the same, act the same, look the same, and say the same things that they say. I would find a conversation with a corpse more engaging than one with the breathing dead, whose next words are as predictable as the liturgy of the priest and who, on pain of death, cannot recall the last book they read. All creativity is dead. All discovery is dead. Feeling is dead. Yet, as we observe, they breathe.

Mankind strikes an unholy bargain at birth. The contract reads: "*Give me life* and I will agree to death." The first freedom, therefore, is the freedom to live in the face of the fear of living and the terror of dying. But such freedom extracts a severe price. The price is pain, the pain of fear—fear of failure, of rejection, fear of abandonment, of loss and of sorrow, and the terror of death. We awaken to find ourselves trapped on a boat floating down an uncharted river with its horrible falls at the end. We possess no map to tell us where we shall face the falls. But we know the falls are there. We know no one ever survives the trip. We are afraid. Yet we cannot get off the river. We can only, moment by moment, attempt to avoid its treacherous rapids, its hazardous back currents, and despite the river's exquisite beauty and its placid bends, often we fail to enjoy the trip, for we know, just ahead, perhaps around the next bend, we shall face the falls, the horrible falls.

Life is the invisible trap. And the invisible tyrant is fear. To many, escape is death. Living death. The trap of the breathing dead is worse than the trap of the coyote whose foot is caught in steel jaws, for the coyote can escape. He need only chew off his foot. But the trap that ensnares the breathing dead tortures beyond endurance, because the trap cannot be seen or touched or even understood. Such traps have no measurable dimensions. When the breathing dead cry out that they are trapped, they are assured that all they need do is work harder, be smarter, compete harder, make more money, and they will, at last, be freed.

Who are these breathing dead? The farmer can be trapped on the farm, trapped by the mortgage that renders him the slave of the banks. The housewife can be trapped behind lifeless, monotonous walls, reduced to slavery to husband and offspring and repressive community mores. The poet, trapped in anonymity, the small-town artist trapped in obscurity, the parent trapped in mindless labor, the child trapped in ignorance and stifled in the great negative mind mill—all can die in their traps before they have lived.

For all creatures who are caught in traps, a sense of hopelessness prevails. At the workplace the breathing dead are not heard, not acknowledged. They are digits on the balance sheet, and digits are dead. Despite what they think, what they say, what they do, or how hard they work, they remain digits. Their protests are like screaming into the void. At the polls they are digits as well, for no matter whom they vote for, nothing changes. They cannot be freed. At last the trap becomes synonymous with life.

But the state of *nonbeing in being* becomes the supreme pain, for eventually it embodies the realization that one has been cheated of his bargain. The breathing dead witness the murder of themselves. The breathing dead live within their own corpses, a horror beyond description, a horror that bears the agony of both murderer and victim and suffers the indescribable pain of the last rejection, of the self against the self.

Alcohol becomes the palliative of choice for the breathing dead. Beer is associated with happiness and is subliminally marketed in place of friendship, as a substitute for love, for sex, especially sex, so that those who thereby escape life through its brown-bottled bubbles are delivered a replacement for genuine joy, and by dulling the senses are delivered a certain quantum of pseudo death. It provides an escape from what appear to be the inescapable traps of life. But the escape is not into the experience of life but the experience of nonlife. So, too, with drugs.

The deadly consequences of food, the most widely abused substance of the breathing dead, are visible in the bloated bodies of the masses and reflect a nation of the entrapped. For centuries we have herded geese into tight pens, held them immobile, and by use of specially devised rods, stuffed rich grains down their helpless gullets until their bellies bloated and their livers swelled, after which we pulverized the livers to produce a delicacy called pâté. In the same way we force-feed geese, the breathing dead force-feed themselves and their children until their guts are distended and their limbs made heavy and stiff like the dead.

Yet many do not so easily succumb. Many strike out in desperate fury. Many strike at anything and everything. They abuse those closest to them, their wives, their children, their subordinates. If they are employers they abuse their workers. If they are police officers they abuse the weaker citizens. If they are judges they exercise their power not in furtherance of justice, but in response to anger, abusing the lawyers who practice before them and the accuseds who plead for mercy.

Hawking substitutions for living has become a massively profitable megabusiness in America. We are provided a love affair with Murphy Brown in order that the sponsor's goods may be subliminally sold in the process. At the same time, we are sold sports cars for sexual potency, shaving lotion for sexual appeal, and shampoo for beauty. Spectator sports provide a substitute for our involvement with our own bodies. Pornography provides an alternative for living relationships, and the pornographic experience mimics necrophilia, since the coupling is with nonliving images on nonliving pages on nonliving screens.

Any commodity that separates people from their lives is in great demand. Television removes the audience from reality. There the mind is redesigned by the electronic god that teaches false wisdoms—that human worth is measured by the amount of money each possesses, that human fulfillment is measured by the numbers of dead objects, gadgets, and things money can buy, most of which are manufactured by the breathing dead themselves in hideous places called factories, where the breathing dead labor with the same low groans and monotonous motions of the machinery. At last, the breathing dead sell their lives an hour at a time to acquire the means by which to buy the stuff of their living death, and when the breathing dead are worn out, like the machinery they mimic, they are written off, cast out, and replaced.

The offspring of the breathing dead are also trapped. Taught by the dead, they learn to say no, not yes, to life, to say no, not yes, to self-expression and exploration. At school, "good" becomes synonymous with "dead." At school most children are not permitted to laugh out loud or cry or make a commotion, because, too often, dead teachers despise any expression of life.

The children's primary experiences, those experiences by which they will make their life's choices and establish their life's values, are not related to clear fishing streams meandering through pristine woods, but to the blood and death and emptiness of life they experience on television. Mindless encounters on the screen waste their lives and dribble away their opportunity for growth. They are forbidden to explore their feelings, for feelings are too dangerous. Their language is not the language of poets but the lexicon of computers. Their heroes are machines and robots and those who emulate the same. They relate more to machines than to peers—to video contraptions that suck in quarters and simulate killing, to driving machines that suck in vast quantities of fuel and carry them endlessly up and down the same streets in a compulsive search for Lord knows what, and to sound machines that in quadruple stereo and exploding subwoofers destroy the ears and deaden the senses.

As are their parents, the offspring of the breathing dead are trapped in the decaying concrete bowels of the cities. The species is not genetically engineered to live where metal machines belch and blow in concrete canyons and fill the air with gases that smart in the lungs, and where the eyes are hurt by the sight of buildings protruding upward like angry stakes. There these concrete children, like rats stacked three deep in a concrete shoe box, begin to strike out. They hurl themselves against the walls, but they cannot escape. At last, desperate to escape, the concrete children can only break out through their fragile selves. Like the coyote in the trap they begin to gnaw on themselves. Crack! Cocaine! Violence! Escape is everything. Freedom is everything. In their madness the concrete children attack their neighbors. The regime calls it crime. But it is only the concrete children searching for freedom.

In a vicious, ever-widening cycle that will surely destroy us, the regime punishes the children by imprisoning them in even smaller, viler boxes of concrete called penitentiaries. We witness a true revolution. It is a revolution against the dead, the living dead. It is a revolution being waged against a dead regime—dead, for its core is composed of a conglomerate of dead corporate and governmental bureaucracies. Included in the regime are those who have become attached to the core, its obsequious functionaries, its glazed-eyed human cogs, its mobs of nodding minions, the endless captured hordes who suck their sustenance from the back of the nonliving beast.

Worse than the living dead, the regime has never taken a breath, never taken a first step or felt a fly on its nose. These bureaucracies are symbiotic and are so similarly structured that if one were to petition the board of directors of General Motors and the governing authority of the Department of Transportation, the responses would be disturbingly similar. What is lacking is the sense that anyone or anything alive—with intelligence—abides within, that there are any living responses buried in any of the vast machinery. The decisions made by the regime could as well have been made by the attendant at the corner Exxon gas station as by the chief executive officer of the same corporation, for the decisions are made by "the book," and the book, of course, is dead. But if "the book" is followed, no one can criticize the decision maker, who in the end makes no decisions at all. Machinery, of course, does not care. Machinery does not think. It does not create. Like an enormous malignant glacier, the regime blankets the earth, consumes the landscape, and leaves its ugly, fatal debris as evidence of its irresistible force.

A dead regime fears its living subjects, for the dead cannot control the living. Only religions have such power. But when the living become the living dead, the equation is placed in balance, for, indeed, the dead can control the dead. Thus freed, the regime may pursue its purpose, namely, to convert all that is living to the dead, to convert clear skies to poisonous dead skies, pristine forests to dead clear-cuts, sparkling rivers and emerald oceans to deadly ooze and toxic silt. When the equation is in balance, the regime can tear down mountains and cut down forests and rip up prairies, transform that which was once of bud and bloom into trainloads of cement, shiploads of lumber, megatons of plutonium, and endless horizons of automobiles and trinkets and junk. The regime characterizes its action as "progress." But the regime's progress is its malignant magic—to transform all that breathes, all that grows, all that is green into dead green—dead green money.

In its insatiable quest for dead green, the regime has punctured the ozone and left the outer layer limp and gaping like a blown-out tire. On a typical day the power regime will destroy 116 square miles of rain forest, about an acre a second. Another 72 square miles will be lost to encroaching deserts. Every day the regime will witness the loss of 40 to 100 species, each of which has been "a pilgrim of four billion years of evolution," and no one seems to know whether it is 40 or 100. Every day the human population will increase by 250,000. Every day the regime will burden the earth's atmosphere with an additional 2,700 tons of chlorofluorocarbons and 15 million tons of carbon. Tonight the earth will have become a little hotter, its waters a bit more acid. By the end of the year the total loss of rain forest will be equal to an area the size of the state of Washington and the expanding deserts will equal an area the size of the state of West Virginia. The earth's human pollution will have risen by more than 90 million. By the year 2000 as many as 20 percent of the life-forms on the planet that were in existence in 1900 will have become extinct.

Fearing the living, the dead regime seeks to confine the concrete children in concrete. But the regime cannot build enough prisons. In the great cities, cities too bombed and broken to fix, the masses swarm. There a bursting discontent, a swelling anxiety, maddens the alienated hordes. Anger is as thick in the air as the heavy, noxious gases. The people breathe in anger and spew it out. They no longer kill each other out of hate. They kill each other because life has been reduced, life is nothing—theirs or their neighbors'—and therefore killing is nothing. Killing has become a nonact.

The concrete boxes in which the children are imprisoned will explode. Already the explosions have begun in Detroit and Los Angeles and in murderous prison riots across the land. They will explode again and again until those trapped within are freed. Nothing can stop the revolution. It is not driven by ideas about good or evil. It does not bow to political axioms, to economic religions, to Marx, or Christ, or money. It is a revolution at the nucleus of being that seeks to free mankind. The genes, in their irrepressible search for life, control. Like a weed chopped down and then chopped again, life continues to force its way upward. Yet for weed and man alike life is painful.

In the cities, where the concrete children terrorize us and themselves, we observe the species now reverted to its raw state of predator and prey. But it is a *living* predator against a *living* prey. The dead regime cannot say as much. Under its power the *dead consume the living*. In the cities the concrete children are both the hunters and the hunted. Despite their envelopment in this desperate meaninglessness, only the living can eventually care for the living. Once more the dead regime cannot say as much, for under its power the living are and always will be but lifeless expendables. In the concrete jungle life is vibrant, pulsing, grimy, painful and dangerous. Fear is the predominant human experience, but the concrete children experience a life that denounces living death even more than death itself.

As the great cities collapse, the children, without choice, without plan, without direction or purpose, will flee. In the same way that an antebellum population migrated from the cotton fields and the plantations of the South to the northern cities in search of freedom, so too the species will return to the countryside, still in search of freedom. Small villages will again prosper. Once more families will know each other. Neighbors will become as tribal members and will again care for each other. There, as with primitive man, the issue will not be death, but life.

Already the inevitable drift from the cities has begun. Millions wishing to escape the war zones have retreated to smaller towns and to the beckoning countryside. The affluent have led the way. It is easier for them. A New York investment banker moves his office to Jackson, Wyoming, and stays attached to the urban body by the umbilical cords of telephone, fax, and modem. A builder abandons his business in Los Angeles and begins anew as a carpenter in Missoula, Montana. A teacher retreats from the rat race and crime in New Jersey and opens an eight-stool diner in Orem, Utah.

The bridge from death to life is built on two tracks. One is the awareness that life is there to live. That life is. The other is the courage to live it—to feel fear, to accept pain, to set the fear of dying against the joy of living. Once life has been slightly perceived, once vaguely experienced, all the boxes, all the concrete, cannot extinguish man's quest for it. That critical, irrepressible yearning, the longing to be free, to be, is at the heart of all that live. The late-blooming bluebell hugs the ground. It grasps the earth's warmth in order to bloom and seed before the winter's freeze sets in. We are touched by the courage of the tender flower. But freedom is born of courage.

In the end, life demands the same courage for living as it does for dying. Every soul who has occupied space upon the face of the earth, no matter how fearful of death, at last musters the courage to die. The courage to live and the courage to die are opposite sides of the same hand. Fear and joy are the opposite sides of the same hand. The hand is life and the hand is death. It is the hand of freedom. It is our hand, the hand that at last can spring the invisible trap.

# 5

# MOUNTAIN CLIMBERS

*The*

*Tyranny*

*of*

*Work*

*A few in this world have not surrendered. No, not yet. They* are the misguided few who themselves are guides. They are mountain climbers by trade, by heart. They think freedom is wealth. They possess no understanding that it is profitless to clutch and claw one's way a few thousand feet up a sheer rock wall and thereafter to rappel down the same wall, only to repeat the identical act a hundred times a year for twenty years running. Mountain climbers cherish gawking at the same sunrises in March, the same new snow on the peaks in October. Each May they long to see the same green curtain come rising up the side of the same old mountains, and some have been known to struggle up a rock wall all day for no better reward than to see the same sunset from the top of the same peak, leaving them to stumble home in the dark as they had a hundred times before. Jaco Red was one of these.

I first met Jaco Red at the emergency room of the hospital in Jackson Hole. He'd helped bring a friend of mine down from the mountain after he'd fallen. A piton had let loose, an old one the climbers had trusted for twenty years. My friend had fallen a long ways onto a jagged pile of scree that lay at the base of the pitch. Jaco Red said when he hit it made a sound Jaco couldn't get out of his ears. Kept hearing the sound over and over. After they'd flown my friend by air ambulance to Salt Lake City I went over to Jaco's place to get the details of the accident.

When I walked in to his one-room cabin I thought of a pack rat's nest. Pack rats don't all gather the same things. Like people they have different tastes that reflect different personalities. You can tell a lot about the little beasts by what they keep around them. Same with men. On the north wall of Jaco's cabin hung a pair of snowshoes, a tennis racket that required restringing, an old calendar picture of a brace of bobwhites and a shotgun, a wall clock in a red plastic case, a bear skull missing a left incisor, a set of white-tail deer antlers, and a single faded moose horn on which had been painted the Tetons at sunset. A battered 30-30 carbine rested on a gun rack fashioned from deer feet.

On the opposite wall, in consummate disarray, hung a rake, a snow shovel, several hammers, a variety of axes, awls, and other hand-tools. On the kitchen table were scattered a harmonica, a banjo, an empty Corona beer bottle, a box of Wheaties amid a pile of dirty dishes. The furniture in the room consisted of a faded, moth-eaten, nylon-covered pink loveseat, obviously retrieved from the city dump, and three wooden kitchen chairs. A greasy frying pan squatted on the stove, and above the stove, on a rack fashioned of baling wire, dangled half a dozen sootcovered pots and pans that had obviously spent many a night over a campfire.

The east wall looked like a direct hit on a spaghetti factory—masses of nylon rope in various stages of life, new, crisp, red coils on pegs, frayed and faded coils of what Jaco called "may-pops" or "snap-in-halfers," ropes kept only for their memories. Next to the rope dangled clusters of "friends," anchoring devices ranging from half an inch to four inches in length, which mountain climbers insert into chosen cracks. They jam them in carefully, precisely, lovingly, implant them tenderly, but not too lustily or carelessly lest the "friend" become irretrievably stuck, depriving them of its dear price, maybe forty dollars, or God forbid that the "friend" jerk loose, as the piton had with my friend, and drop them in a long, fading scream after which nobody would look down because they knew what they would see. Next to the "friends" hung wedges of aluminum, a sixteenth of an inch to an inch in diameter, called "stoppers," that snapped open and closed to accept ropes and slings and belt loops and which, in a crisis, also opened beer bottles.

Several old wooden crates containing Lord knows what—the family album, perhaps, snapshots of lovers now faded on both film and memory, of people once young and sleek and wrinkle-free when life still held its promises—were stacked on the floor of the cabin. There was poetry in those crates. I knew that—mountain climbers all wrote it, those misfits caught in eternal adolescence, those naive mountain monks who believed in the goodness of man and saw life as valuable and things as rarely relevant unless they could get you up and down a sheer rock face. They believed that the experience was *it*, not some predacious goal sought in panic, not personal power, not money—certainly not money.

Life itself was a free-fall through space that celebrated the quality of the anguish one felt, the style in which one bore pain, with or without tears, the grace with which one experienced joy, deeply and silently, or by letting it fly in great yodels across the canyon walls. These mountain climbers believed in a natural justice, in karma, but they never said so, and few ever experienced justice, natural or otherwise. Yet they never surrendered. No. Not yet.

They wrote more poems. They wrote about the mystery but not about the meaning of life, which somehow escaped them. They wrote about nameless streams that descended from the high meadows like gleaming threads of silver, about the teeth marks of beavers in old tree stumps and the wetness of grass and the darkness of dead falls. They wrote of hiding, of discovery, of a marauding mother moose and lost springtimes, and of avalanches that had taken out a friend like a fly smothered in spilled soup. They wrote of lost loves, because their women raged, and their women begged, and their women wept, and their women always left them. And they wrote of despair, of hanging on in lonely nights, and they also wrote of fires in the hearth that were chilling fires, and the sounds in the room that were silent sounds. But they had never surrendered.

These mountain climbers built their lives on faith that it would all work out, that they would at least be loved, at least accepted, at least not hated, at least not attacked and maimed. At least not killed. And some were maimed, some killed, and some nearly starved to death as they gladly, even fervently, sacrificed their youth to perfect a difficult move on an overhanging cliff a thousand feet above the ground, or only five feet above the ground—it made no difference—for no one saw their triumphs. Mostly they never spoke of their successes to anyone, and in return they expected that no judgments be leveled against them, at least no criticism, at least that no charges be filed, at least no convictions returned—at least not banishment, nor demand for surrender—well then, at least no order to deliver up their souls in retribution for their crimes. The likes of Jaco Red climbed rock. They climbed something solid, something connected to the stars, but the mountains they climbed were composed mostly of themselves, and they had never surrendered. No. Not yet.

And then to feed their bellies that grew lean and shrunken and accustomed to the regularity of irregular feeding they compromised, as we all must compromise, and they became mountain guides two-and-a-half months a year, and joined the search-and-rescue teams for which they received shameful pittances. These men, who took the lives of the rich and the famous and the whiny, tender sons of the wealthy into their hands, were paid less than baby-sitters, less than the pimply-faced kids at McDonald's, and they lived in small huts at the Climbers' School and scraped by. When they got sick no one called the doctor, and when their mothers died, they did not send flowers. They sent a small note, for they understood that their mothers could read the note as well as they could smell the flowers. "I know you now understand, Mom." And they called on certain mysterious forces for replenishment, and they also felt the perverse joy of not having surrendered. No. Not yet.

# 6

# THE NEW KING

*Tyranny*

*of the*

*Corporate*

*Core*

*A small troop of alien explorers, visiting from a distant yet* uncharted planet, allegedly recorded these chilling observations concerning the sanity of "Earthlings." If nothing else, their recently discovered papers make interesting reading:

> These Earthlings are insane according to their own definition—*a disassociation from reality.* Existing in nearly total fantasy, they murder each other over imaginary icons and destroy entire segments of their societies over beliefs founded in myth. Nowhere in the universe have we encountered such an abdication of reason than among the natives on Earth.

I can, of course, make no claim for the veracity of these reports, and I attribute to them no more credence than one might to Mark Twain's *Letters from the Earth.* Yet their purported view of us is curious, if not amusing:

However, Earth provides a valuable laboratory by which to study the phenomenon of "teachable psychosis." Earthlings instruct their offspring that various myths are fact, that certain fables are historically true, that diverse fictions and fairy tales must be believed, thereby rendering entire populations, by definition, mad. Heretofore we had believed insanity to be the product of infirmities of the central nervous system, but our observations of these Earthlings have demonstrated that *insanity can be taught*, that the psychosis that predominates the Earth is, in major part, a phenomenon of programming, a process the Earthlings themselves understand metaphorically as "brainwashing."

Admitting only for argument's sake that we are, indeed, suffering from some sort of bizarre social psychosis, the earth explorers have given no consideration whatever to "freedom" and the effect its enjoyment or its depravation has on the human condition, for if the body of human desire is the pursuit of happiness, freedom is its soul. Yet the alien explorers themselves seem to have long ago rejected freedom as either a definable or useful social notion, for, irreverently, they refer to freedom as "one of the Earthlings' most profoundly peculiar concepts. . . ." Their report makes the following comment:

Although the term "freedom" eludes precise definition, for what seems to be freedom for some becomes tyranny for others, yet quite inexplicably these Earthlings fight for freedom, die for it, make speeches about it and even celebrate a day in its honor, all the while understanding little if anything about this elusive notion. Moreover, many believe they are free when, in fact, they are bound in the most abject servitude imaginable.

If, as alleged by the alien explorers, we suffer a form of taught psychosis, then may not such teaching also be untaught? If the brain can be soaked in the brine of myth and madness, may it not also be soaked in clear, pure waters of truth and enlightenment? At last, does not freedom begin with a mind washed of beliefs, for if we believe in the teachings of one demagogue have we not locked the door to all other possibilities? At last, does not any belief become an encroachment on our right to inquire, extract from us our right to choose, and therefore diminish, our freedom? In sum, the world is full of either believers, who have no proof, or doubters, who, having proof, disbelieve it.

Nonbelievers, the heretics of history, were burned at the stake. In America, today's heretics, those who refuse to accept the religion of "free enterprise," are burned otherwise, usually with labels that serve the purpose of modern inquisitors just fine. Our miscreants are labeled as "far left," "knee-jerk liberals," "Commies," "tax-and-spend liberals," "tree huggers," and the like. The labels ostracize, and although we no longer burn our dissidents at the stake, our method of eliminating them is as effective. If candidates for public office raise issues that threaten the power structure, we unearth the women to whom they have made love and expose them as lechers and liars. If people oppose the power base by rioting, they are imprisoned. If they oppose the power base by passive resistance, such as those who refuse to pay taxes on moral grounds, they are held up as kooks and weirdos and are also imprisoned. If people wish to expose the corporate oligarchy for the crimes it commits against the people, they are silenced, usually not by violence (although Karen Silkwood's fate seemed an exception), but simply by isolating them from the public media so that the rest of the people are not permitted to hear them. As in the days of the Inquisition, the crime is still heresy and the punishment is still banishment, if not by death, by separation from the community and nation.

The power of the system to banish its aberrant

members is usually rooted in the belief system of the majority. A million women in history could not have been burned at the stake absent a culture's insane belief in witches. In our time, a nation of women could not be subjugated by a male-dominated society but for an equally insane belief in the exclusive right of men to wield power. Hitler's insanity could not have been imposed on millions but for the insane support, passive or otherwise, of an entire nation. Worldwide, it is a chilling spectacle to witness hundreds of millions of people clutching opposing economic and political dogmas, both of which tend to enslave their subjects. The earth explorers commented on one side of this phenomenon as they observed its operation in the United States:

> In furtherance of our conclusion that Earthlings suffer bizzare aberrations of the mind, we report the following: There exists on earth a host of controlling entities called "corporations." However, try as we may, we have been unable to demonstrate that these entities are alive, that they breathe or feel or that they physically exist. These corporations appear to have no life as we understand life. They seem interested in but one thing, a lifeless paper symbol that measures the worth of all things and all Earthlings—something Earthlings call "money."
>
> Although corporations do not breathe, they are said to breathe money. Although they have no blood, their blood is said to be money. Although they have no brains, they are said to think money, and although they have no visible mouths, they speak only in terms of money. Although corporations do not live, their lives are devoted to the gathering of money, and although they are soulless, their souls are said to be composed totally of money. It remains an enigma to us that any but the insane could devote the labor of their entire lives to such non-beings. By means of the corporate-owned media, closely censored information is disseminated that portrays the corporate oligarchy as honest and just and also con-

vinces the people it is proper for non-living entities to own or control the entire wealth of the earth while the living should be allowed only that which "trickles down." So convinced are the Earthlings of this religion called "free enter-prise" that they willingly lay down their lives and the lives of their children to protect the oligarchy that continues to exploit them.

Americans have always suffered a severe emotional allergy to the idea of a monarchy, the evil said to have prompted the American Revolution itself. That America is governed by an oligarchy of mammoth corporations is a fact readily observed by the alien explorers, a fact, however, that would enjoy little acceptance in any quarter in this country. The aliens thought it remarkable that Earthlings should be ruled by a nonliving conglomerate of corporations the aliens referred to as the Earthlings' "New King." Here is how they put it:

> ... the people are not aware that a New King reigns. They are vaguely cognizant, of course, that there are clusters of monstrous corporate entities that seem to control them, but they are no more sensitive to the ubiquitous nature of their enslavement than they are of the unrelenting pull of gravity. In fact, they seem to unconsciously fear their independence of these corporate entities, this New King of theirs, in the same way they might fear the loss of their subjugation to the gravitational pull of the earth—that if gravity were extinguished they might suddenly find themselves flying free with no means by which to affix their feet to the soil.

We are assured from birth until we draw our last raspy, mortal breath that we are a "democracy," an integral but mythological part of our belief system that we take on faith. Plato thought that a democracy was "a charming form of government, full of variety and disorder, and dispensing a sort of equality to equals and unequals alike." But Plato would not have been as amused were he to visit America. Here he would have discovered a rather orderly, compliant people bemoaning the fact that there is still not sufficient order and compliance. He would, to his dismay, see that the only place people are in actual control is in the streets, where ruffians and gangs predominate while elsewhere the corporate collective controls. He would fail to recognize our government as a democracy but would view it as a sort of hybrid, exhibiting all the elements of anarchy one day, those of fascism the next, a government that sounds like a democracy at election time and operates during the rest of the year as a capitalistic oligarchy through endless government and corporate bureaucracies. He would observe that the government is run by people who, on Monday, work for various bureaus that supposedly regulate the corporations but who, on the following Monday, are employed by the same corporations that, the week before, they had regulated. He would see a gaudy patchwork quilt that creates a state never before seen, heard of, or imagined in the history of mankind.

In this crazy quilt the aristocracy is the aristocracy of "old money," of inherited wealth, that is the American equivalent of inherited titles. The quilt has its socialistic patch evidenced by Medicare, workers' compensation, and Social Security. It displays a patch of the monarchy in that the underlying, nearly absolute control of the nation is handed down from generation to generation of banks. On this crazy quilt Plato would clearly see a patch that looks and feels like communism, since the major functions of the government are, as in the communist nations, operated by deeply embedded, hopelessly entangled bureaus where nothing is accomplished because the function of the bureau is to intercept every living idea and to smother it. To be sure, Plato would recognize a democratic patch as well. It forms a bright star in the center of the quilt, but its function is mostly to provide the rhetoric enjoyed on the Fourth of July and during election years, when then, and only then, the people are courted and coddled and told how important they are.

Franklin Roosevelt warned that "the liberty of a democracy is not safe if the people tolerate the growth of private power to a point where it becomes stronger than their democratic State itself. That, in its essence, is Fascism, ownership of government by an individual, by a group, or any controlling private power." Bombarded as they are with such noise and hullabaloo pronouncing their freedom, the people cannot hear the thief steal into the house. Upon such evidence, democracy seems to be a fine form of government so long as the people do not engage in it.

In place of a democracy we have accepted as an article of faith that we live in one. In order for corporate power to remain in power, the illusion of freedom is crucial, and lip service is, therefore, faithfully given to the democratic ideal as surely as the priest kisses the holy chalice. The seemingly incurable affliction of democracy is that, as practiced, it has not succeeded in delivering democracy.

We elect a new president or install another party not because the people, independently, have chosen to exercise their power, but because the New King has not been prospering. Whereas the beneficence of the King only dribbles down, his misery is shared by the bucketsful. When the New King suffers, there is all hell to pay. He clears his court. People are laid off by the millions, usually at Christmastime. The streets are filled with the confused, the wandering, and the helpless. Still the people turn to the King and listen to the King, who incites their passions not against himself, of course, but against the King's men, the politicians. That "the King can do no wrong" is at the heart of English common law, and although the English kings have delivered their thrones to the museums, the idea of sovereign infallibility, when the sovereign is the nation's capitalist central nervous system, is still deeply embedded in America.

As William Penn once observed, "Let the people think they govern and they will be governed." An illustrative cartoon shows a puppeteer, representing the moneyed power structure, with a puppet on each hand. First the puppeteer raises his right hand and the puppet squawks and carries on and eventually it withers and falls. Then the puppeteer raises his left hand and again the puppet obediently performs and fades away. Alas, the puppets take the stage and depart at the whim of the puppeteer, who, himself, never makes an appearance. And although we sense his presence, we see only his performing hands and hear only his voice disguised in ways to mimic our own.

*We are told that our judges, charged with constitutional* obligations, insure equal justice for all. That, too, is a myth. The function of the law is not to provide justice or to preserve freedom. The function of the law is to keep those who hold power, in power. Judges, as Francis Bacon remarked, are "the lions under the throne." Our judges, with glaring exceptions known to all, loyally serve the New King, the corporate core, whose money and influence are responsible for their office. They are not bad people. Indeed, they are among our most upright citizens, although few have written a poem, painted a picture, or sung a happy song.

As righteous and honest men and women, although mostly dour and humorless, they faithfully serve the law and, accordingly, the King. They restrict the power of the people, usurp the power of the people's juries, and reserve the people's courts chiefly for two functions: to provide the means by which the people are imprisoned for their crimes against the King, and to provide an administrative forum for the King to carry on its commerce, most often the multitudinous aspects of the insurance business.

Today the courts are choked with lawsuits brought by people against the New King. When they sue each other as a result of an automobile accident they in fact sue the King, for both parties are likely insured. When they sue an employer for their injuries they also sue the King, for their employer is also covered by insurance. When they sue a newspaper for libel for having besmirched their good names and reputations, again they sue the King, for again the newspaper carries insurance. When a doctor cuts off the wrong limb or ignores obvious symptoms and the patient dies, if suit is instituted, the King is concerned, for the doctor, too, is insured. And if the lawyer who brings such suits is negligent in his services to his client, at last the King is still the principal party, for the lawyer carries malpractice insurance as well.

Steadily the courts have become mere clearinghouses for the insurance industry. The courts establish the myriad hoops and hurdles people must negotiate in order to obtain justice, and since justice for people's injuries, their deaths, damages to their persons, their reputation and property is measured in money, and since the money comes from the invisible pocket of the King, it is unlikely that many will receive much. Seen from the perspective of the insurance industry, the courts have become extensions of the insurance companies' claims departments, since the courts determine which claims will be paid and the terms of such payment.

A problem endemic in a system that imperfectly protects the interests of the New King is that some judges are actually enlightened, even idealistic. Some are largely guided by human conscience. Some of the more innocent judges take their oaths of office seriously and believe that justice, whatever it is, should be rendered as often as possible to the people. I think of the great judges of the Warren Court. I think of Justice

William O. Douglas, who once had the audacity to suggest that even trees had standing in the law. I think of Rose Bird, who assented to her demise as chief justice of the California Supreme Court rather than vote for the execution of the wretches imprisoned in death row in response to the obscene argument that it is cheaper to kill them than feed them. And what of Brandeis and Holmes and Hand and Cardozo? What of Judge Miles Lord who, against the most virulent personal attacks of A. H. Robins Company, enforced the rights of multitudes of women injured by the Dalkon Shield? What of the countless judges in the wayward communities of this nation who have devoted their lives to the cause of justice?

Yet perhaps these great judges have done more to impair our freedom than to free us, for their faint light that shines through the melancholy mist of the judiciary has caused us to focus on them rather than the darkness that otherwise surrounds them. Who remembers Chief Justice Taney of the United States Supreme Court, who held that the black man, Dred Scott, was an "ordinary article of merchandise?" Who remembers the endless series of justices who have been more interested in their golf games than the suffering of abandoned wives and hungry children? Do we recall the judges by the trainloads who repay their political benefactors with their decisions and turn their black-robed backs on the injured, the forgotten, and the damned?

One is hard-pressed to find a judge these days who is not a former prosecutor of the people or a former corporate attorney who, as a judge, takes his experience, his loyalties, his training, and his prejudices with him when he is elevated to that high place. Show me a man who, as a lawyer, made his fortune in service to corporate clients and I will show you a man who, as a judge, exhibits a mind and soul still bent in the same direction. One cannot feed from the corporate trough for thirty years without developing a certain predictable kink in the judicial neck.

In the federal system judges are appointed for life by those who hold power at the pleasure of the New King. After their appointment these judges answer to no one. Presidents may come and go. Congress may be cleared out and cleaned up. But the judges live on. Whole generations of citizens may be born and buried, but one can look up and behold the same judges occupying their august and gloomy thrones. Dealing in human misery—the wresting of children from their mothers' breasts, committing the poor and the ignorant to those dank and dreadful holes called penitentiaries, dealing with every offense, evil, and deviation known to man—must provide nourishment for judges, for they live on and on and endlessly on. One judge has more power than all the people put together, for no matter how the people weep and wail, no matter how desperate, how deprecated and deprived, a single judge, wielding only the law, can stand them off. Judges are keenly aware of their power, and power, like the reproductive muscle, longs to be exercised.

Judges can commit nearly every variety of injustice that satisfies their whim or caprice of the moment. I have known judges who at 10 A.M., while still suffering from their daily hangover, would sentence a felon to life imprisonment. Yet the same judges, after their noonday toddy, might release the same felon on parole. Worse is the intellectual and moral lethargy judges demonstrate year after year with empty, droning opinions—opinions without meat or bone that leave the people starving for justice. Judges can go crazy—indeed many seem mad—but unless they are foaming at the mouth and tearing their robes into small pieces, they are permitted to send men to prison, to deny the helpless their just dues, and to interpret the laws of the land.

When a quite ordinary lawyer is elevated to the position of judge, once in the robe, seemingly by magic, this ordinary person is transformed into the rarest of the species, one of unusual insight and infallible wisdom. His once-worn jokes suddenly become hilarious, her merest suggestion a command. We now address this person as "His Honor" whether or not what His Honor does approaches anything honorable at all. Worse, the judge who may have been no more than a blinking bumbler among his peers, shortly after donning the robes, finds himself also believing that his ascension into the rare air of the bench has magically endowed him with a new and immense intelligence, a deep and unquestioned sagacity.

In the "state court system," the judicial selection process is even more bizarre. There, the judges are elected by the people. But since these judges are paid a pittance—the real compensation being the honor and the power they enjoy—and since they must obtain a majority of all votes cast to obtain or thereafter retain their offices, many must expend large sums of money to gain and hold office. Often, therefore, they accept contributions from the very lawyers and litigants who will later appear before them.

Our visitors from outer space also made comment on our methods of judicial selection:

> . . . strangely, these same Earthlings would riot in the streets if politicians appointed the umpires for their baseball games in the same manner that their judges gain office, especially if the appointments were for life. And they would storm the capital if the referees of their football games were elected by the team owners, and the owner who contributed most to the referee's campaign got the best calls at crucial moments in the game.
>
> Our observations convince us that judges in the United States are chosen not for their love of justice. While those who maintain a fondness for art may paint and those who are enraptured by music may play the violin, those who love justice

rarely become judges. In fact, judges, by their acts and utterances, demonstrate daily that they hate justice and despise people.

How do we preserve our freedom with judges who have been ensconced in their high places by The New King or who are otherwise beholden to those who appear before them? Our judges should be drafted in the same manner that jurors are drafted—to act as judges for a limited calendar of cases after which they would be released to return to their practices. Every trial lawyer should be required to support the system in this fashion the same as every citizen is required to serve as a juror. If judges were drafted from the trial bar we would soon clear our dockets, because we could call up as many judges as were necessary to bring our dockets current. If judges were drafted, we would no longer be saddled for life with the political cronies of those in power, or be faced with judges who have received campaign contributions from our opponents. To be sure, we would experience some bad judges. But, Lord knows, we have them now—and often for life! On the other hand, we would benefit from the best minds in the legal business, who, under our present system, rarely seek the judiciary.

*I cannot think of a more deserving group to be placed in the* public stocks of public opinion and whipped than lawyers, but if we are to reap any benefit from the whipping, lawyers must be criticized for the right reasons. The clear gist of the nation's antilawyer campaign is, of course, simplistic: If Americans can only get rid of the damnable lawyers our medical costs will go down, our courts will no longer be jammed, our criminals will no longer escape through those legal loopholes, we will all have dirt-cheap insurance, the stockholders of the insurance companies will reap record dividends, and we will live happily ever after. Lawyers are blamed by politicians for whatever goes wrong, by law-enforcement officials who, embarrassed, cannot by honest means convict those charged with crimes, and by insurance companies who have made bad business investments and must answer to the stockholders for their woeful quarterly profits.

But blaming lawyers for all of society's ills is like blaming doctors for all of our physical ills, our mental disorders, and the fact that our indolent backsides have grown wider. We would likely not further our health interests by raising the hue and cry, "Kill all the doctors!" In a legalist system, in which, indeed, we struggle, lawyers are the only profession dedicated to preserving our freedom, although they are not very good at it. Lawyers have been portrayed as slithering rats in the alley—squealing, shrieking, screaming, snarling, ripping, and tearing at everyone, everything, and each other over every scrap of garbage. But there is a strategy of the nonbreathing regime. It is to cause us to hate and despise those who might be able to save us. If a nation distrusts its lawyers, who is to stop the New King? If a nation spurns its warriors, who will fight the wars? Who, pray tell, will protect our rights?

Assuming that there existed in this country an adequate fund of well-trained advocates, which we shall see is not the case, the King takes the first cut, in the same manner as if the Super Bowl champions were given not only the first draft choice but all succeeding drafts until they could draft no more, leaving the scrubs, the cripples, and the midgets to play for the opposing teams. I do not suggest that there are no great lawyers who represent people. There are a few great people's lawyers in the country like there are a few great judges. But most of the greatly skilled trial lawyers in this country are in the service of the corporate core.

Populated by professors who are, themselves, unskilled in the trial of cases, law schools teach the law like one who teaches cooking but has never fried a flapjack. It is an astonishing spectacle to see a professor strutting in front of two hundred or more dull-eyed students lecturing, say, on the law of evidence, when the professor himself has never looked into the face of a single person accused of a crime. It is equally bewildering to learn that law schools turn out thousands of lawyers each year, most of whom have never seen a contract, never drawn a will, never filed a simple petition in bankruptcy, and never drafted a complaint for divorce. Indeed, most have never spoken to a live judge or even know where the courthouse is.

Rather than deploying "the best and the brightest" into the far nooks and crannies to protect us from the tyranny that threatens us, our "best and brightest" are sold to the highest bidder among the large law firms who, after retraining them in any of hundreds of legal subspecialties, unloose them together with others of their kind against the people in much the same way that hounds are turned after the rabbit.

Although, strangely, doctors find the rich more needful of medical care than the poor, doctors usually ply their skills to the health and well-being of their own species. We would find it bizarre if our best and brightest doctors, after receiving their education at medical schools we support, devoted their lives to the health of our most feared enemies while, in turn, we could find no doctors at all when we broke our legs or ruptured our bellies. And what if the great minds of medicine stood in attendance during all of their professional lives to a variety of nonliving monstrous entities that enslave us? Under such circumstances would we think them quite mad? Would we not cry, "Kill all the doctors"?

When citizens must face Goliath, who confronts them as corporate employers who have stolen their rights, when citizens must face gargantuan insurance companies who refuse to pay their just claims or, in the hell of all hells, when they must stand up to the monstrous power of government that threatens their very lives, where do the citizens find their David? Most will sorrowfully discover that it is impossible to find a lawyer whom they can afford, who is trained and qualified, and who will throw his very body and soul into the fight. Little wonder that when the citizen cannot find a good lawyer, he comes to the belief that all lawyers are bad.

How can we know justice if our young are not trained to fight for justice? We can train football players and doctors. We can train people to cook the culinary fares our bellies crave, but for some reason we cannot seem to train lawyers to preserve our freedom. We should run most academicians out of the law schools. We should train our lawyers like we train doctors. They must learn their skills by practicing them under the supervision of those who have already acquired them. On their first day in law school they should begin to learn the skills of advocacy. On their first day in law school they should begin to learn that simple caring for their suffering brothers and sisters of the human race is the most important gift any lawyer can give.

Our law schools should be experiences in how to deliver justice, not esoteric exercises that teach our young how to play word games. Our lawyers should be chosen like we choose athletes. We do not choose athletes for their ability to solve word puzzles but for their ability to perform, for their courage, strength, their will, their stamina. Neither should we choose our lawyers because they can satisfy a computer-driven test such as the LSAT. Such a test separates those who possess a certain measurable mental agility from those who do not. As a consequence we end up choosing mental types who can please a computer, without regard to their ability to care for and fight for people. Lawyers should be chosen because they can demonstrate a history rich in human traits, the ability to care, the courage to fight, the will to win, a concern for the human condition, a passion for justice and simple, uncompromising honesty. These are the traits of the lawyer. These traits cannot be measured by computers or by computer-driven tests.

Our young should be trained to fight for justice, not to scorn it in the style of their professors, most of whom adore free-floating intellectualizations but seem to care little for people. If there is one thing that is obviously wrong in America today, it is the endless flooding of our country with young lawyers who have been kissed by a computer, chosen not for who they are, but for the word puzzles they can solve, and who are dumped on the public sorely lacking any experience in the true skills of lawyering.

In America the cost of justice, even in the simplest of cases, is prohibitive for ordinary citizens to bear. Insurance companies that stand behind most of the litigants in the major money cases in this country encourage their hourly paid lawyers to take endless depositions, to file every motion contained in their computers full of motions, and to otherwise doggedly resist the payment of just claims. Their lawyers religiously shun settlement opportunities and continue the harassment of the injured until the last drop of their fees has been squeezed from the bloody turnip. Insurance companies are almost religious about it— they would rather pay a million to their lawyers than a thousand to the father whose child was run down by the drunk the company insures.

On the other hand, when individuals decide to sue a corporation they can usually afford to do so only by pledging a portion of their recovery to their lawyers for their fee. Under such circumstances only the best and easiest cases find representation, for unless the lawyer can win he does not get paid. The small but important case, the new or novel case, the case of principle with little damage, the just but difficult case, the case requiring the investment of large sums of money for witnesses and research—all are cases likely to be lost for want of a lawyer, leaving multitudes of just cases never to see the inside of a courtroom. The winner, by default, is usually the King.

When a citizen is charged with a crime and cannot afford a lawyer, one will be appointed for him, not because the system is essentially fair, but because to retain the confidence of the people, the system must *appear* fair. Usually the defendant's lawyer is one freshly popped out of a law-school factory somewhere and has had little, if any, experience in the courts. But the contest proceeds nevertheless. I would rather watch the ant engage the elephant in mortal combat than witness the usual unequal matches between the government and the individual. Guilty or not, most people charged with crimes give up and plead guilty.

A federal prosecutor is often the most powerful individual in any community, even more powerful than the judge. He can prosecute the judge. In fact, he can obtain an indictment before a grand jury against anyone he chooses. When the grand jurors meet, the evidence presented to them will be double and triple hearsay and will consist of all manner of other incompetent allegations. The proceedings are secret. Secret! In many jurisdictions it is a crime for the grand jurors or any witness to divulge what evidence was presented to them. If you are the target of the investigation, you are not permitted to have a lawyer present to protect your rights or to help you tell your side of the story. The only lawyers present are the prosecutors themselves. No judge is present to restrain the prosecutor, who presents the evidence he chooses and argues as he pleases. Little wonder that, as the saying goes, "a grand jury will indict a ham sandwich if the federal prosecutor asks it to do so."

One has never experienced the power of the federal government until one encounters the FBI, the investigative arm of the federal prosecutors. Few defendants are fortunate enough to have any money left to engage the services of a private investigator after they hire their lawyers, but the government puts scores, even hundreds, of agents against the defendant on important cases. They probe and pry into every conceivable wrinkle and crevice of the defendant's life. If you have erred, if you have angered anyone, if you have failed in any way, they will discover it and bring witnesses to court to prove it. The findings of the FBI laboratory at Washington, D.C., have become synonymous with scientific fact, and whether you are guilty or not they will find a fingerprint, a hair, a flake of skin, a voice print, semen, something, that can be attributed to you. And often, whether you are guilty or not, that is the end of the story.

If you are charged with a crime and are dragged into court in shackles, suddenly you become a member of that vast mob of criminals that we all fear. Even though you are innocent, *we will fear you.* And we will love the cops and the FBI, who have become our new heroes, for, as is demonstrated daily on the King's television, they risk their lives on our behalf against the likes of you. We already know who is guilty—the one with the shackles, *you!* Otherwise you wouldn't be in court. And we know all about your lawyer, as well. He's one of those grease-laden shysters who will try to squeeze you through some legal loophole that remains unplugged.

Not only do we presume the accused guilty, but any experienced criminal defense lawyer will tell you that his client is usually tried in the newspapers and convicted long before the case begins. The FBI, the witnesses, the prosecutors themselves, step before the cameras, tell their stories, show the booty, the guns, the drugs, the blood and the gore, and if you are the accused they look into the camera with honest eyes and in plain talk connect the fruit of the crime to you. Many veteran trial lawyers are convinced that although the government still gives lip service to the jury system and to our constitutional rights, trials have largely become public trappings to reinforce the myth that in America we are still free.

Although we profess to be a civilized nation of law and order, we still execute our criminals for the exact crime we commit against them. When a person murders, his crime is punishable by death, but for a collective of persons called "the State," to murder the murderer becomes no crime at all but is merely punishment. Our explorer friends made comment on this matter as well:

> We find it difficult to understand, indeed, we think it further evidence of deep social psychosis that Earthlings believe they can punish their murderers for murder by murdering them. Moreover, since death provides a release from the pain and punishment of life, how can death be punishment? Earthlings can only punish the living, not the dead. Yet they still persist in killing the living as punishment. When Earthlings murder a murderer, strangely they punish his innocent family, his grieving parents and his horrified children who must bear the pain and the shame of his execution. The murderer is not punished. We have never heard of a dead Earthling complaining or crying out in anguish, or begging to be forgiven or, at last, admitting he has learned his lesson. And if punishment is intended to teach, how do Earthlings teach the dead unless, of course, they believe that in their next lives they will remember and do better? It is entirely incomprehensible to us that the justice of Earthlings should finally be reduced to the government mimicking the forbidden acts of the criminal. That is to say, when the criminal kills, the state kills in kind.

*Today we live in a world where all we encounter are* potential predators, not members of our flock. Our leaders are liars and cheats; our representatives, bought and sold; our bankers, crooks; our clergy, money-hungry charlatans; our businessmen, frauds; our screen heroes, deviates and dopeheads; our neighbors, robbers and murderers. Once tribal animals, we have lost the security of the tribe. We no longer enjoy the comfort of our families, who have been scattered across the land in search of employment. Paranoid, terrorized, and alone, we scurry and hide in the concrete jungles while the King further convinces us with the King's television voice that our true enemies are ourselves.

Witnessing the reported and dramatized crimes of our species against ourselves, we rarely obtain a clear view of the crimes of the King against us. As estimated by the Bureau of National Affairs, the dollar cost of corporate crime in America is over ten times greater than the combined larcenies, thefts, robberies, and burglaries committed by individuals. Since the savings-and-loan scandals, that estimate has more than doubled. The theft, embezzlements, and money laundering of our leading investment brokerage houses and banks is staggering proof that, although we rob and mug each other and break into each other's houses, although we cheat and steal from each other and defraud each other of our property, our crimes are of the magnitude of shoplifting to a Brinks robbery compared to the King's crimes. Although to hush the hue and cry of the people, the New King is required to take token action, the crimes of the corporate core go essentially unpunished.

But if the earth explorers were bewildered by our views on capital punishment, they were utterly dumbfounded when it came to our punishment of corporations.

When punished, the corporation never repents. Nor is it jailed, for, as we have observed, these corporations do not exist in any physical sense so they cannot, in fact, be punished. As concerns justice, those invisible entities are, for reasons not at all clear, in most ways above the law and remain immune to the operation of justice.

Yet, justice itself was treated by our visitors from outer space as an archaic notion that had little practical application in their way of things. The alien explorers commented on "this strange notion" as follows:

> If a child is born in misery and filth and grows up to commit miserable and filthy deeds, the child is punished, we presume, for his misfortunate birth by being imprisoned in even filthier and more miserable cages called "penitentiaries," all of which Earthlings command in the name of justice.
>
> If an Earthling, a member of a hungry minority, robs a grocery store, he is cast into one of those infamous penitentiaries. But if a corporate bank robs the people of their life's savings and squanders billions of their dollars, nothing happens to the bank at all. Instead, if the bank fails, the people are required to save it by contributing to it through more of their life's earnings in what they call "taxes."

But the real crimes of corporate America are not crimes punishable by law because the corporate power nucleus does not tolerate laws that unduly inhibit its quest for profit. Therefore corporations have remained free to convince our young that it is "hip" and "in" to smoke, thus insuring the costly and agonizing deaths of generation after generation, while other corporations profit from the care of the victims in corporate hospitals at exorbitant prices.

Corporations demand that our workers labor in unsafe workplaces, and lie about the efficacy and safety of the drugs they market to the desperate and the ill. They spill their oil on the land and in our oceans and mock the people when called upon to make restitution. As public utilities, they overcharge their customers. As mine operators, they tamper with samples of respirable dust taken to protect miners from lung disease. As operators of thousands of nursing homes across the land, they drug or tie down their helpless patients in order to save the cost of adequate attendant care.

The list of horrors, of corporate excesses and wrongs, that critically affect the lives of every citizen in America is endless. When a corporation's crime is discovered and the corporation sued, secret court settlements allow the offending corporation to continue to take its profit from the same killer products that brought them to court in the first place.

A few years ago a family was driving along on a peaceful Sunday afternoon when a driver, still drunk from the night before, came over on the wrong side of the road and crashed head on into their car. The car burst into flames, and when the occupants tried to escape, they found to their horror that all the doors and the windows were jammed shut from the impact. Before the family burned to death, the mother, with superhuman strength, was able to break through a window and throw her son clear of the car. There on the ground, horribly burned, the child watched helplessly as flames consumed his family.

When we investigated the case, we learned that the manufacturer of the automobile, one of America's major corporations, had conducted crash tests proving that when the car was involved in a head-on collision, a flange in the gas tank would break and gas would leak out, often catching fire. Although this defect could have been easily remedied at a cost of only a few dollars per car, the company put a pencil to it. The company's moneymen computed the cost of defending a few lawsuits, and the probable jury's awards, compared to the cost of correcting the defect in the gas tank. Profit won out. To put their decision in perspective, they knew that people would likely die but there was profit in letting them die.

If we were to profit for killing another person, we would be treated as killers for hire and executed. But when the corporation kills for its profit, rarely is anyone punished. The corporation paid only the amount required to secretly settle the case with the child's guardian who, faced with the child's enormous medical bills, was forced to take the secret settlement. In the meantime, the number of innocent people who have been killed by this napalm bomb on wheels remains a buried secret.

Little organized resistance is leveled against the New King in this country today. We have become compliant and domesticated. Unions are said to have outgrown their usefulness, although the rank and file suffer the worst conditions at any time since the founding struggles of labor. Rightly, we are continually reminded of our abuse of our children, but we are told little of the abuse of our children in the reemerging sweatshops of the King. The New King has a more subtle touch. No longer does the King loose the police and National Guard against its strikers and murder them by the scores. Strikers are simply fired and replaced. Competition with Japan, where human rights has been even less of a national concern, has caused the New King to advance the notion that America, to be competitive, must emulate the paternalist attitude of the Japanese toward labor without regard to the fact that such paternalism was the underlying force of America's pre–Civil War enslavement of African-Americans.

As children we are taught the difference between right and wrong. We develop consciences. The chief executive officer of one of our great American chemical companies would never think of dumping his garbage on his neighbor's front lawn. But his company dumps dioxin in the rivers that belong to all of us. He and the corporations of his fellow CEOs, many of whom share each other's boards of directors, unremittingly pump chemicals into our air that then descends upon the earth as acid rain. Every minute of every day, millions of decent people perform indecent acts on behalf of the corporations for which they work, acts they would never commit in their own names. People are the tools of the corporation, not vice versa. If corporations were merely the tools of people, as some argue, we ought not give rights to tools. And if we did, we would not pit a D-9 Caterpillar tractor, an obvious tool, against a child shoveling in his sandbox.

Of course, corporations are owned by their shareholders. Pension funds own stock. Schoolteachers and doctors own stock. But corporations are principally owned by other corporations, and corporations are usually controlled not by the stockholders but by managers who neither own a significant portion of the stock nor answer to anyone who does. Corporate management these days is like a bird on the back of a galloping steed. The bird has very little control of the horse, is there mostly for the ride, and can fly off whenever the horse stumbles and falls.

In the days of the black slave, a relationship, although often unspeakable and heinous, existed between master and slave. Master and slave were chained together. Neither was free. Evil as the best of these relationships were, they were nevertheless human relationships. The slaveholder, if he had a conscience, had to answer to his conscience. The slaveholder, if he had a soul, had to recognize it as his own. Cruelty and exploitation were carried out face to face.

But what about this new master of ours? We are chained, but by invisible chains to nothing. We are enslaved, but when we fall sick and can no longer work, we are retired without enough to support even our dignity. Across the land our corporate masters employ every trick, every connivance, to cheat millions out of the pensions they have earned in exchange for having contributed their lives to the New King's profit. Like chickens in the chicken coop, we believe we are free. We can squawk and crow all we want; we can fuss and fight and strut and screw and compete for the scraps the farmer throws us, but we are still in the chicken coop. And the farmer gets the eggs.

I think of the loyal employees of a large steel company at its plant in a small western town. They were an older work force who had labored long and hard to make certain that their plant was profitable, having been assured by management that profitable plants would remain open while those that were not would be closed. Moreover, they were promised by the highest officer in the corporation that under any circumstances their plant would remain open for several years to come. Then suddenly the plant was closed. Several thousand workers faced devastating crossroads in their lives—unemployment, early retirement, loss of pensions. When the smoke cleared in litigation, the court found that the corporation had intentionally broken its word to its workers, because in doing so it could avoid the accruing pension benefits it had agreed to pay them.

It is commonplace in America these days for corporations to strip their employees of their hard-bargained-for and dearly earned pensions and other benefits as a part of the King's insatiable quest for profit. Profit is everything. The never-ending search for profit transcends all moral considerations. In fact, profit is the ultimate moral imperative, the first and last commandment in American business. That companies should break their word to thousands of people who believed them, that they should cheat employees of their just dues, and that countless workers should suffer and despair are of little consequence. Numbers on the bottom line, not principles of right or wrong, dictate the consciences of most corporations. Indeed, the bottom line *is* their conscience.

Since corporations have no souls and no commitment to the human race, corporations will always commit wrongs in their unquenchable quest for profit. The corporate structure may be a necessary evil to gather the capital required to carry on business, but the corporate structure, itself, is inherently evil. It is evil in the same way that a person without a conscience is evil. Psychologists call such persons "sociopaths." Our most cold-blooded killers are usually so classified. Manson is a sociopath. Dahmer is a sociopath. Many times I have seen these wretched creatures with their empty eyes sitting in the courtroom as the state's psychologist explains to the court and the jury that somehow they have been cast into this world without a conscience. There is no guiding mechanism to keep them from committing wrongs, and science has not yet devised a means by which to graft a conscience onto them. But we can graft a conscience onto our mammoth corporations.

Every large corporation should be required to seat on its board an equal number of ordinary people, people who have no pecuniary interest in the corporation's activities, who will act as the corporation's conscience and who are selected at random from the tax rolls of the community in which the corporation carries on its principal business. These "conscience members" of the corporate board will see that the rights of the corporation's employees are preserved, that their pension funds are not raided, that the workers receive fair wages, that their benefits are equitable, and that the corporation acts in accordance with every standard of good citizenship.

Corporations should be held accountable to people in proportion to their power, for power, of whatever magnitude, demands a corresponding quotient of responsibility. We do not hold the dependent child to the same level of responsibility as his more competent parent. We do not hold the family pup to the same level of responsibility as the child. Yet people often exercise responsibility far out of proportion to their power. Take Sam Jones, for instance. He runs the local filling station. First off, he obeys the law. He respects his neighbors. He does good and charitable works—coaches Little League, and cleans up the barrow pits of the highway near his town. He works extra hours to put his children through school, serves on the jury when called, gives to the United Fund and his church, and supports a community project for the homeless. Why, then, shouldn't the corporation that supplies the gasoline that Sam sells, that profits from Sam Jones's labor, and whose financial power is several million times greater than Sam's, also be responsible in proportion to its power?

Shouldn't that corporation strictly comply with all our laws? Shouldn't it be acutely aware of its responsibility toward its neighbors, making certain it does not dump its pollutants on them? Must it not serve the many communities it touches in the same fashion that Sam Jones serves his? Shouldn't that corporation reinvest its moneys in these communities in proportion to the gross profits derived from each? Shouldn't it take part in the education of the communities' children, granting scholarships to those in need, as Sam has educated his? Shouldn't that corporation provide the community the wherewithal to improve the community, just as Sam has?

I am, of course, aware that corporations undertake various altruistic deeds. But in size, they bear about the same proportion to the corporation's total financial ability as the gnat bears to the camel's back. However, as usual, the corporation zooms in on the gnat. During half-time of a college football game we learn on television that some large American corporation has given a thousand-dollar scholarship to each of the schools involved, the cost of telling us about this gift being hundreds of times greater than the gift itself. Giving was not the issue. The opportunity to exploit the gift was. It is an unquestioned axiom of corporate policy-makers that to give money away is irresponsible. One of my friends, the former chief executive officer of a large American corporation, told me, "No honest corporate executive would think of giving his shareholders' money to charity. We are not a charitable institution. We are a profit-making institution." Even though the Internal Revenue Service permits corporations to deduct charitable contributions up to ten percent of their taxable earnings, corporate giving has always remained around the one-percent mark. A conscience grafted to a corporation would cause it to take part in and care for the community just as Sam Jones takes part in and cares for his.

In the end, a corporate conscience would prove good for business. Employees who are happy, who are treated with respect as persons, not as digits, not as expendable rags, will produce more. Corporations who act responsibly will be viewed by the consumer with a more tolerant eye. If corporations were responsible we would have less need for the host of government bureaus that are said to so inhibit corporate activities: the SEC, the FDA, the FCC, the EPA— The list covers scores of pages—agencies, mostly ineffectual, designed to keep corporate America honest. If corporations were more responsible, people would resent them less and sue them less. Indeed, corporate planners have acknowledged for many years that corporations can actually increase profits by acting responsibly. Why then don't all corporations become fully responsible citizens in the communities in which they do business? The answer lies in the *nature* of the beast.

I once had a dog named Buster. He was a chicken killer. No matter what I did to old Buster I could not cure him of killing chickens. But most every rancher in the area had a sure-fire cure for chicken killers and I tried all of their remedies.

One neighbor held that dousing a chicken with Tabasco sauce and turning the dog and the chicken loose in the chicken house was a guaranteed cure. It didn't work. Buster paid the price, but he got his chicken. Another neighbor said I should put a muzzle on the dog and lock him up for a week in the chicken house, letting him out only to eat and to drink. I tried it. As soon as I took the muzzle off, Buster was right in the middle of the chickens again. Still another neighbor said I should tie one of the chickens Buster killed to his collar and make him drag it around for a couple of days. I tried that too. But Buster's commitment to chicken-killing remained immutable and his lust for their blood insatiable.

Finally I came to an obvious realization: It was Buster's *nature* to kill chickens. I finally gave Buster to an old boy down the road who owned three other dogs with the same incurable propensity. The neighbor hated chickens himself, he said.

Corporations, as a phenomenon, would rather exploit than contribute even if, in the long run, contributing would result in their amassing greater profits. It is in their nature to exploit. But we can change the corporate nature. We can make corporate officers as well as employees both civilly and criminally liable for all violations of the law. If the human agencies of corporations were held responsible for the corporation's acts, a workman would refuse to violate the law for fear the crime—say, dumping pollutants in the river—would be chargeable against him, and the corporate executive, for the same reason, would refuse to order the dumping in the first place.

*We have been skillfully sold the idea by corporate America* that if social programs were eliminated and taxes lowered, everybody who is willing to work would benefit and those who have previously laid back and drained the system would be made to carry their fair share. The idea was that if corporations and individuals alike had equal rights and proportionately equal burdens, everyone would live happily ever after. By this device the wealth of the country has been redistributed over the course of but two presidencies resulting in the most severe atrophy of the middle class since the Industrial Revolution.

I remember the story about five mice and a hog who were shipwrecked on an island so small there was barely room for all of them. On this island a single source of food existed, a coconut palm that grew at the water's edge. At first the mice and the hog fought over who should have what portion of the coconuts as they fell. The hog, being the larger, took all the coconuts, but the mice, being nocturnal, pestered the hog while it tried to sleep until at last the hog was required to strike a fair bargain with the mice.

"Logically and fairly," the hog said, "and we are fair and logical creatures, we should divide the coconut in accordance with our respective weights."

"But we would get practically none of the coconuts," the mice protested.

"Yes, but you don't need very much, while I need a great deal to maintain my strength against the waves that dash against this little island."

At last the mice, having little with which to bargain and being unable to assail the logic of the hog, agreed, and the coconuts were divided according to the animals' respective weights.

As time went on, all parties strictly honored their agreement, and although the mice appeared to prosper, the hog prospered also. But as more time passed the hog grew fatter and fatter. Although the mice had sufficient nourishment, the hog finally grew so large that there remained room on the island only for him. The mice one day could not retain even the tiniest toehold and thereupon were finally crowded off of the island, fell into the sea, and drowned. The moral of the story, of course, is that fair bargains are often likely to do you in, especially if you are as small as a mouse.

*In similar fashion the corporate King uses another tenet of* our religion against us—our right in a civilized society to be free of fear. The argument that ultimately further enslaves us feeds on truth. True, we are robbed in the streets and we are afraid to go to our cars after dark for fear we will be mugged. True, we do not feel safe in our homes. We bar the windows and doublelock the doors. True, today we are as likely to spend our money on burglar alarms as vacations. People are shot in the street without rhyme or reason. The cities are out of control, and the criminals who bring all this terror down on us seem to escape through endless legal loopholes. If we were dealing with poisonous rats and rabid dogs, we would plug the holes through which they attack us. And, as the argument goes, so must we plug the legal loopholes that permit the escape of our criminals.

But these so-called legal loopholes turn out to be our sacred rights. When we destroy the rights of our enemies, we also destroy the rights that protect us. We know that. But deep inside we believe that our neighbors—someone else, not us—will suffer a heart attack, or experience the terrorizing ravages of cancer. And it is someone else, not us, who will need the protection of our constitutional rights. After all, only crooks get crossways with the law.

But what happens when it's our child who is arrested? Then we will mortgage our homes to bond him out of jail and we'll deliver our life's savings to one of those infamous criminal defense lawyers to protect our child in court. When we discover that the search was conducted without cause or without a warrant, but that the objects seized will, nevertheless, be used against him; when we discover that his confession was coerced but it will, nevertheless, be used to incriminate him; when we learn that criminals have given perjured testimony in exchange for their freedom, but that our child will, nevertheless, be convicted by their testimony; when we learn that the state has withheld evidence tending to show that our child was innocent, but that, nevertheless, the jury made its decision without having heard it; when we discover that the state is free to violate most of our child's rights because judges are no longer independent, faced with charges, as they are nowadays, of being "soft on crime;" and worse still, when we learn that our child, once in prison, has lost most of his rights as a human being and can be raped and in nearly every way abused, even killed, by inmates and guards alike, perhaps then we will remember that the loopholes that we have plugged prevented our child from receiving justice.

A new tyranny has cast its cold and ugly shadow over the nation, a nation where the rights of the people, criminals and citizens alike exist mostly in myth, where the police have become the handmaidens of power, where trials have become mere window dressing and mockeries of justice, and where corporations are left free to pillage and ravage the people with utter impunity.

*We are not a democracy, nor have we ever been. I have in-*sisted we are more nearly a corporate oligarchy. Corporate money elects our presidents and selects our congressmen, our cabinet members, and our judges. Corporate money has bought the country. And the question that begs answering is how to remove the near total control of nonvoting corporations and return it to voting citizens.

The ancient Chinese thought that no leader should be permitted to seek power. They believed that those who seek power *need* power, and that those who need power ought not be entrusted with it. I agree. Moreover, the perennial complaint expressed by nearly every citizen at election time is, "Why, in a country of over a quarter of a billion people, can't we come up with candidates better qualified than these?" Many citizens, in deep disgust, refuse to take part in the electoral process, believing that to do so dignifies the mammoth hoax being foisted on us.

Plato argued in his *Republic* that our representatives should be selected at random from the whole population, that from a fund of all qualified voters we simply draft our representatives. Those whose names come up in the selection process would be required, by law, to serve. By this method we would draw as many women as men. More poor and middle-class representatives would be chosen than those who are economically privileged. We would have proportionately as many members of minorities as exist in the whole population. Indeed, by such a process of random selection, we would obtain a house that truly represents the demographics of the nation.

These representatives would serve one term—perhaps four years. During their term, they would receive an adequate salary and the jobs they left would be protected by law. A representative committee selected by the body from the body would choose our candidates for president—presumably the best qualified men and women in the country—those with the best history, the best experience, the best training— the very best that America has produced. Such leaders would have values consistent with those of the people themselves—that people, not money, that justice, not profit, are the first considerations, that progress is realized when we feed and house and educate our citizens, that progress is realized when we preserve the earth. These candidates, so selected, would be drafted to stand for election. And the people, after they had been fully informed concerning their qualifications, would select one of their number to serve as president for a single term.

Some observe that such a method of selecting our representatives bears with it the danger that some will not be qualified to represent us. But we have survived in a system for over two hundred years where most who represent us are either not qualified or are committed to interests antithetical to our own. I find it easier to trust the schoolteacher or the bulldozer operator over the professional politicians I have known. I would more readily trust the waitress and the high school custodian to know more about right and wrong than any I know who occupy high seats in Washington. This great cross-section, like jurors, would bring to government a knowledge of the human condition not often found in the elitists who hold office, and this great cross-section would terminate forever our representatives' pathetic indenture to the power of the money that hoisted them into office.

This selection process puts our view of democracy to a true test. Either we are a democracy, and as a consequence we are willing to vest the people's power in the people themselves, or we are not. Either we believe people are qualified to govern themselves, or, at last, we must admit that we do not believe this at all and that our preachments to the contrary have been only a part of a cruel and deluding two-century swindle of our freedom.

To be sure, despite its manifold defects, we love our country. It is ours. We make our living here—a better living than most people elsewhere in the world. We pride ourselves in being Americans. We zealously guard our rights to engage freely in commerce, to realize a profit, and to speak and write freely. We are patriotic, loyal to our country and to the ideals it symbolizes. When faced with the system's faults we may acknowledge them with a shrug of the shoulders and reply with the old cliché, "The system may not be perfect, but it is the best system ever invented by man." But suppose medicine had been satisfied with such an argument concerning, say, infectious diseases. During the time of the Continental Congress, doctors went from one patient to another without scrubbing. They operated with filth and infection dripping from their hands and spread disease from one victim to another in vicious ignorance. But the operations they performed, although not perfect, were the best known procedures of the day.

We can do better. Yet, like any conscientious doctor, we must first diagnose the diseases of our society. The first step toward freedom is to recognize our enslavement. Indeed, our system may be the greatest in the world, but to those who are forgotten by the system, for the over 25 percent of the children of this country who go to bed undernourished, the system is not good enough. There may be liberty and justice for all—for all who have not sought it in the courts—but for the woman who cannot support her children because she has been discriminated against at her workplace; for the citizen who cannot feed his family because he does not have sufficient education to compete in the marketplace; for the worker who cannot retire because he has been cheated out of his pension; for the innocent who must walk the plank of no return through the monstrous criminal justice system; for the people who are lied to and cheated, who are poisoned; and the earth that is polluted for profit—for all of them, who at last become all of us, the system is not good enough.

I do not argue for a sharing of the wealth. I do not endorse Marxist principles that, when put in practice, have too often obliterated the very freedoms they guaranteed. But neither can one embrace the religion of Free Enterprise when freedom in that context means that *nonbreathers* are given unlimited license to squander the resources of the world, to turn the living earth to a dead and poisonous crust, and to possess the wealth of the earth while the masses of mankind struggle and starve in invisible shackles.

Wealth at last is translatable into cans of beans and blankets. Wealth is translatable into life, into health, and to freedom. We would think it madness were we to visit a man who had already acquired ten square miles of canned beans, the cases of beans stacked twenty stories high, with an endless train of trucks laden with yet more beans entering the compound while the compound itself, always expanding, was protected by a surrounding fence and thousands of guards to keep the starving outside.

"What are you doing?" we might ask the Bean Man. "Can't you see people are starving?

"This is free enterprise," the Bean Man might reply.

"I know, but you can only eat so many beans. And, after all, you can't take the beans with you."

"I'm leaving the beans to my kids. Besides, I use beans to keep score. That's my hobby. I'm a bean counter."

"What do you mean 'keep score'?" a pale, gaunt woman in rags asks through a crack in the fence. "Can't you see that my child is starving?"

"Go to work," the Bean Man says. "I worked for my beans, you work for yours. And don't forget, I'm giving ten cans of beans to the scholarship fund of my university next month." Then he orders one of his men to board up the hole through which he hears the woman, and after which he cannot hear the remonstrations of the mother or the whimpering of the child, for all he can hear is the sound of his own voice as he continues to count his beans.

That corporations, like the hog, should acquire *more* and *more*, just *more* for more's sake, while the powerless of the world do without food or shelter or education or medical care, at some point transcends reason and mocks justice. Such evils can be accepted only as we accept the injustices of any religion. We accept such injustices on faith that our religion is inherently just. But *more* merely for more's sake is not free enterprise. More for endless more finally becomes madness.

In its perfect state, free enterprise calls upon the human species to rise to the divine. Above all, it demands freedom. Its soul is the soul of freedom. It strives to free us so that we may exhibit our grace, our creativity, the fruit of our love, indeed the product of our virtue. It frees us to inquire, to explore, to pursue the muses of both art and science. It permits us to chase our dreams, different as they may be from our neighbors'. It lauds our blessed individuality. It allows us not only to acquire our needs but to fulfill our avaricious longings. Yet free enterprise never contemplated that the ant should compete for survival against a herd of stainless steel elephants.

The conclusion of the alien explorer's report read as follows:

> We began our observations concerning the Earthlings by suggesting they were insane in accordance with their own definition. No better evidence of their insanity exists than when we inquired into their views of "success."
>
> Earthlings pity the person with an insatiable appetite who as a result of his disorder becomes so obese he can no longer waddle even to the dinner table. But they laud those who suffer from a similar greed for money. They shun those who are sexually insatiable, referring to them as "satyrs," "sluts" or "nymphomaniacs." But those with an insatiable craving for money are held in the greatest esteem. Those who are addicted to alcohol or drugs are treated as ill and seen as socially unacceptable, but those who are addicted to the endless acquisition of wealth are endlessly admired.
>
> Money also is seen as a desirable substitute for most other worthy human traits. For example, an ugly person with money is often coveted as a mate whereas an ugly person without money is

usually not, leading us to conclude that money stands for beauty. A dishonest person with much money is more likely to obtain a loan of more money than an honest person without money, leading us to conclude that money stands for honesty.

A dullard who never exhibited an original thought in his life, but who has money is more likely to be found in the higher echelons of the system than a person with original and startling ideas who has no money at all, leading us to conclude that money stands for creativity. A product that sells for more is considered to contain more intrinsic worth than a better product that sells for less, leading us to conclude that money stands for quality. An artist whose work is common and mundane but who can exchange it for money is considered a better artist than one whose creations are original and unique but who cannot sell his work, leading us to conclude that money stands for taste.

Those who have money are considered wise, while those who have little are often thought to be fools, leading us to conclude that money stands for sagacity. Those who do nothing but permit their money to earn money are considered to be virtuous while those who have no money and who pursue none are often considered lazy.

Stranger still, those who are born with money rarely produce anything of worth but are yet considered worthy, while those who acquire large amounts of money are usually as dull and uninteresting as money itself. Yet one with money will be listened to even though he squawks like a chicken while poor poets go unnoticed. If one steals a little money he is considered a common thief. But if one steals huge amounts of money he is considered a successful business man. *Indeed, these Earthlings are insane.*

Yet the species displays a divine connection to the light and grace of the universe. Their poets and artists are inspired though little heard. Their tenderness can be as pure and perfect as the bloom of the lily. Their love can be passionate, their courage the courage of the gods. They are both mechanical and spontaneous, lifeless and creative, insensitive and exquisitely aware. They can hate and adore with equal force. They can be both intelligent and inexplicably obtuse. They can be maddingly objective or objectively mad, it being beyond our ability to predict which trait will be evidenced at any moment. Albeit they are quite insane, they are, indeed, most remarkable and charming creatures.

*By reason of having been born on this earth, human beings* are endowed with certain inherent rights, no less divine than those of a squirrel who acquired similar rights when it was born in the forest. By natural law squirrel and man alike are entitled to sufficient food and adequate shelter. By natural law the squirrel possesses its hole in the tree and is provided the opportunity to fill its nest with nuts. I confess I have never seen a hungry squirrel. If man, indeed, rules the earth, why then should the human creature be entitled to less than any of the other members of the Society of Creatures? Is not something quite awry when man, allegedly the most intelligent, the supposed occupant of the highest place on the totem, grants himself less respect than the squirrel or the mouse?

Anthropologists insist that native man, the hunter and gatherer, labored less than an hour daily to acquire his food. Were he judged by today's standards we would proclaim him indolent and shiftless. Yet his ability to provide for himself was in direct proportion to his freedom. He was not the unwitting slave of *nonbreathers.* He lived with the *living,* related to the *living,* lived with and for his *living* family and his *living* tribe. Poverty was not yet discovered. The magical forces of money by which man exchanges his virtues for that which is intrinsically without virtue were yet unfamiliar to him. That for two million years primitive man should have provided food and shelter for himself and all the members of his tribe, while civilized man with a vastly greater ability to do so has not, suggests a social sickness yet to be attended to. That civilized man strives mightily to build enough new penal facilities to house the bulging criminal population and does little to house the innocent homeless suggests a social aberration yet to be confronted.

When nature is properly in balance, everything growing is respected. The squirrel may become food for the owl, and the fawn, food for the wolf. But neither owl nor wolf stack up corpse after corpse in front of its lair to keep score. The respect of creatures for creatures is founded upon the natural law that recognizes that all life is interdependent and is thereby entitled to dignity and respect. The similarity of the ideals of free enterprise to the jungle have often been observed. But in nature, the laws in place do not permit the children to destroy the mother, or to say it otherwise, the occupants of the earth to destroy the earth itself.

By virtue of having been born, every child in this country, indeed, on the face of the earth, is entitled to the same rights as the squirrel. Such child is entitled to a decent shelter over his head and adequate food to nourish her growth. Under natural law every creature is afforded the opportunity to fulfill its genes. The fawn grows into the majestic buck and runs as fast and jumps as high as it can. The hawk grows to soar as high as its great wings will carry it. To the same extent, every child born is entitled to an equal freedom, an education that provides the opportunity to become the best that the child can be.

We have the ability to eradicate hunger and eliminate poverty. We have the ability to give our children their just dues as members of the Society of Creatures. We suffer only from having abdicated our moral commitment to do so and thereby we have abdicated our membership in the Society of Creatures.

But at last we are free. Our knowledge frees us to

make our choices. We may join an insane order where mankind has been relegated to the lowest position on the totem, where, at the bottom, he and his children are tormented by hunger, where his freedom and the freedom of his children have been lost and replaced by an empty myth of freedom and where man has become subjected to an insidious servitude to the New King, the collective corporate core, that abides outside natural law, or we may cast off our invisible shackles.

I have made it clear I do not argue that mankind should share the wealth. Nature does not create man or any of its other creatures with equal needs, equal drives, equal talent, or equal responsibility. I only argue that we are, like the squirrel, created with an equal right to *our natural entitlements,* to adequate food, adequate shelter, an equal right to grow and to bloom, and an equal right to dignity and respect as members of the Society of Creatures. After every member of the species has enjoyed his or her *natural entitlements,* plenty remains for the acquisitive to squabble over.

The goal of the New King is to subjugate the earth and its population to the most insidious tyranny ever experienced by man, a tyranny that is guarded with a religious zeal by its very victims, who mouth the dogma of the New King's system with such slogans as "with liberty and justice for all," and "government of the people, by the people, and for the people." It is a tyranny with a state religion. The religion is Free Enterprise. It is a tyranny supported by the people as their sacred right, one that enslaves the people while it convinces the people they are free.

In the end we need not despair, for natural law will prevail. The sick, the deviate, the mad, cannot long survive. In their place a new and healthy entity, a new and vibrant village, a new and caring community, a new and progressive free nation, will take their places. A species that cannot control its populations, that cannot feed its masses, that cannot educate its children, that cannot respect its members, that cannot curb its greed, that cannot worship justice over power, that cannot reject evil over good and death over life, will in due time correct itself, since all life is finally subject to natural law. And the sooner we submit ourselves to such law, the sooner we and our children will know freedom.

# 7

# THE NEW INDIANS

## *The*

## *Tyranny*

## *of*

## *Poverty*

*Freedom, like painting, like music and dance, is irrelevant to* the starving. The dancer cannot dance with a body benumbed in a sweatshop. Children who are frightened cannot sing. The species, hungry and exhausted, must attend first to the body; freedom is a matter of the soul.

I remember when as a young cowboy, I found a horse tied by a stout halter to a fence post. No food or water or any human habitat was nearby. The horse was too weak to lift its head. Its ribs were showing. It was obviously dying of thirst, and it was starving. I rode on, thinking that the horse belonged to someone who had tied it to the fence and would soon return. But when I rode by again that evening the horse was still there. I stopped, slipped the halter off the horse, and freed him. Shortly I met a man riding toward me on an old plug that was plodding along with its head between its legs. The rider, an evil-looking sliver with a dirty beard and a black sweat-soiled hat, pulled up as we met. He carried a 30-30 in a saddle scabbard. As the man spoke to me through brown teeth we were in sight of the starving horse.

"You turn that horse loose?" he asked.

"Sure did," I replied. "Looked like somebody left him there to starve."

"I left him there," the dirty sliver said. He put his hand on the butt of his Winchester. "I tied him there for a reason."

"What would that be?" I asked.

"On account of the fact that I'm tryin' ta break the bastard to ride. This here horse is his full brother." He gave the plug a jerk with the reins. "And he was jus' like 'im. Couldn't even get a saddle on the bastard much less get on 'im. But ya starve 'em down a little, and they'll do damn near anythin' ya want 'em ta do. They learn fast, hungry." He laughed.

"How long's that horse been tied there?" I asked.

"Week, little better maybe. I took him to water once. Now I gotta go catch the son-of-a-bitch 'cause you went an' turned him loose. I oughta make you go catch 'im."

"You won't have any trouble catching the horse," I replied. "He's too weak to run."

"Good," the sliver said. "He'll be jus' right to put a saddle on." Then he gave his horse a vicious kick in the ribs with his spurs. "An' I better not catch ya stickin' yer nose inta my business ag'in," he warned. He patted his rifle butt, gave me a brown, wicked grin, and rode off.

I think of John Brown, the spiritual leader in the great Civil War, who struck against the system on behalf of his black brothers and sisters. But few of the masses in bondage rose up to follow. As in most wars, only the radical edge, the impassioned few, responded. The mute majority, gagged by hunger and poverty and silenced by fear and ignorance, are heard to mumble only occasionally from under their rags in the dark of night.

Today the starving hordes in Africa appear weaker, hungrier, and more desperate than the horse I found tethered to the fence post those many years ago. They are mostly silent. Some of our children in the ghettos fare little better. As the children grow up on the streets they find ways to fill their bellies and gain respect among their peers, usually by methods repugnant to us—gangs, drugs, crime—mostly crime against each other. Then we feed and house them in the penitentiaries. Today the number of African-Americans in our prisons exceeds the slave population of the South at the time of the Civil War.

But slaves in chains have always understood they were slaves. Black American slaves worked nearly naked in the cotton fields on little food—a handful of corn a day that they ground and baked over an open fire after laboring from dawn to dusk—no meat—and sometimes they were whipped, without mercy, for small offenses. But what of the people who are told they are free—but cannot get jobs? What of the people in America, the land of the free, who are trapped in slums, in filth and poverty, whose children go to bed at night hungry? For many, the differences between slavery in the old South and entrapment in today's ghettos are confusing. People who are hungry cannot understand freedom, and people who live on the streets can only search for a grate upon which to survive one more bitter night.

Yet as has been clearly demonstrated since their invention, man can survive in his desperate traps. Man can exist in crumbling ghettos, in appalling concrete camps. He is a creature well adapted to pens and penitentiaries, and he can breathe the blue and yellow gases until his lungs shrink and his muscles shrivel. Among creatures, man is very tough. I have seen the streets, empty except for blowing paper and an emaciated dog lying in the center of the roadway too weak to move. The "can boys" had already come and gone.

They were old men who salvaged the aluminum tins from the garbage and traded them for cheap wine, and ate whatever scraps they could find, rotten or not. The dog could not compete. The can boys were free, of course, but humans cannot claim their freedom when their stomachs are cramped in hunger and their lives are only embarrassing blots on the cover sheet of the Bill of Rights.

I remember the beet workers' shacks in Wyoming. They were less habitable than the ranchers' chicken houses. I have seen the hovels of the poor caving in on the banks of polluted rivers. I have turned my head for fear of what I might see inside. The slave quarters of a hundred years ago were probably as livable. To-day's ghettos may be worse, the bricks crumbling, the dark stairways caving in, the broken walls covered with graffiti, mimicking buildings shelled in a war zone. I have seen people cold or, in the summer, sweating in dirty sheets, sick, often worse than sick. If such places became the kennels and stables of our animals, we would object out of common humanness. In fact, by gross number, most of the human species lives where only rats and roaches prosper. And humans entrapped in such places do not devote much time to notions of freedom.

I think of the zoo's polar bears, who also live in concrete. Although the bears are fed, the hair has been rubbed off their bellies, leaving them as red as wet meat. The visiting children do not see the bears' belly, and the sow aborts most of her young. And eats them. Like our cities, the polar bears' cage has no fence around it. Fences spoil the illusion of the bears' free-dom. Instead, a deep pit entraps the bears in the same way that a pit of poverty entraps the ghetto's human occupants and separates them from the rest of the system.

To be sure, "freeways" provide easy access in and out of our cities, but for many, there are no free ways to freedom. If we were to construct a bridge across the polar bears' pit so they could escape their cage, they would likely scurry back, for the polar bears know no other place. The cage is their cage. What the bears lack, those entrapped in the ghettos also lack: a vision of freedom.

I should think it difficult for our concrete children to imagine a grove of quaking aspens in the Rockies where yellow warblers blast the summer's silence with joy. I should think it equally difficult for them to conceive of the Great Plains, where on a clear day you can see a hundred miles. I should think it hard for them to believe they could be walking down Fifth Avenue as an editor in one of our great publishing houses or a lawyer arguing a case in court. In short, our children's poverty includes a terrible poverty of vision.

"You are free," the schoolteacher tells her class.

The hungry child does not reply. In New York City there are ninety thousand children who have no bed of their own, children who are housed in rows of cots like skinny, featherless chickens in a chicken coop.

"You are free," the schoolteacher says again. "That is important to know."

Still the child does not reply. Liberty, like radishes and parsnips, does not flourish in impoverished soil.

The social and economic dynamic that denies freedom to those who most require it flourished conspicuously at the time of the American Revolution. The energy of the revolution was supplied by large landholders, slave owners, and wealthy merchants, by men who were members of the colonial ruling class. The revolution was not fueled by the masses, by the hungry and disenfranchised. George Washington was the richest man in America. John Hancock was a prosperous Boston merchant. Benjamin Franklin was a wealthy printer. Even Thomas Paine recognized that money and liberty were somehow inextricably connected.

In *Common Sense,* Paine wrote, "I challenge the warmest advocate for reconciliation to show a single advantage that this continent can reap by being connected with Great Britain. Our corn will fetch its price in any market in Europe, and our imported goods must be paid for by them where we will.''

John Adams, who argued for a republic, was at odds with Paine, who leaned too far in the direction of pure democracy. Adams denounced Paine's plan as ''so democratical without any restraint or even an attempt at any equilibrium or counter-poise, that it must produce every evil work.'' A legislature of riffraff could not be kept under control. Adams thought such an assembly would be ''productive of hasty results and absurd judgments.'' But as the revolution progressed, even Paine made it clear that he was not in favor of empowering the masses. He had become an associate of one of the wealthiest men in Pennsylvania, Robert Morris, and in the end supported Morris's creation of the Bank of North America.

The rights of man, yes, but the rights of man to his profit—that was the driving force of the American Revolution. Slogans like ''No taxation without representation'' were appealing and right. But the revolutionary leaders distrusted the mobs of poor who inhabited the land. Although slaves accounted for 25 percent of the population and in some counties as much as 50 percent, their freedom was not a significant factor in the revolution. Washington refused to emancipate blacks in exchange for their joining his army against the British. But on the British side, Lord Dunsmore promised freedom to Virginia slaves who would join him. This caused much concern. Moreover, poor whites were continuously encouraging slaves to run away. One county in Maryland reported the situation as follows:

> The insolence of the Negroes in this county is come to such a height that we are under a necessity of disarming them which we affected on Saturday last. We took about eight guns, some bayonets, swords, etc. The malicious and impru-

dent speeches of some among the lower classes of whites have induced them to believe that their freedom depended on the success of the King's troops. We cannot therefore be too vigilant nor too rigorous with those who promote and encourage this disposition in our slaves.

But the slaves did not rise up.

And what of the poor whites? Many sold their services to the wealthy for a pittance, some for as little as five pounds and a little porridge, and, standing in stead of the wealthy, they were wounded or killed as soldiers in Washington's army. Alexander Hamilton, an aide of George Washington and a member of the new elite, wrote from his headquarters: "Our countrymen have all the folly of the ass and all the passiveness of the sheep. They are determined not to be free. If we are free France and Spain must save us." Indeed, it was the French who came to our aid. The British chalked up victory after victory until the end, when the Americans, aided by a large French army and with the French navy blocking the British from their supplies and reinforcements, won the final battle of the war at Yorktown in 1781.

Freedom then and now seems more at ease in the company of the affluent. Our own Declaration of Independence omitted mention of important groups— native Americans, slaves, and women were conspicuously left out of that great document. One paragraph of the declaration even condemned the king for inciting slave rebellions and Indian attacks:

He has excited domestic insurrections amongst us, and has endeavored to bring on the inhabitants of our frontiers, the merciless Indian Savages, whose known rule of warfare is an undistinguished destruction of all ages, sexes and conditions.

Although Jefferson was the owner of more than a hundred slaves, he had originally included a paragraph in the declaration accusing the king of bringing slaves to America from Africa and "suppressing every legislative attempt to prohibit or to restrain this execrable commerce." But the paragraph was stricken by the Continental Congress, because slaveholders themselves could not agree on the question of that infamous business. At last, slaves, mostly hungry and afraid, became irrelevant.

Freedom, like a concern for the environment, is a luxury. In the same way that freedom is irrelevant to the hungry, so is the earth's preservation an empty cry to those without jobs. Joblessness creates an unholy alliance between the living, who must love and respect the earth, and the dead corporate King, who is bent on destroying the earth for profit. People must work, but more and more their work compels the injury or destruction of their mother earth.

I have seen felled firs covering an area the size of a hundred city blocks and stacked as high as tall buildings, some of which were already mature trees when Thomas Paine and Thomas Jefferson were expounding on the rights of men. But forests have no rights. Men, on orders from their corporate employers, clear-cut millions of acres of virgin, old-growth forests, whole universes of flora and fauna, of ferns and cover for the blue grouse. Men, on orders from corporate bosses who have never set foot in any forest, much less a virgin, old-growth forest, chop down the nesting limbs of the brown thrush, and destroy the refuge of elk. They rip up the mulch and the soil in which grow the yellow columbine and the scarlet Indian paintbrush. They devastate a world where ten thousand different species of bugs and beasts and bloom once lived in balance and in harmony. But people need jobs.

I do not argue that we should not build houses of lumber. But there are thousands of empty houses across this continent rotting and wasting. I argue that our forests are managed as tree mines and that America's corporations that chop down and grind up our forests are subsidized by our taxes, for, as is well known, the cost of delivering our forests to America's corporations far exceeds the revenue those same companies pay for the timber they harvest. Much of our timber, of course, is shipped to Japan, an island without great forests. There the people cut our lumber into small pieces and cherish it. There our lumber is sold at great profit, and there our lumber makes jobs for the Japanese.

I think of our native Americans who cut from the forest only what they needed—a few dead saplings for their tepee poles, roots of certain plants, and the fruit of shrubs. When a woman cut the roots of a young cedar tree she was heard to pray, "Look at me, friend! I come to ask for your dress . . . for I am going to make a basket for lily roots out of you. I pray, friend, not to feel angry with me. . . . " The forest did not know when the Indian came or left. On the prairies Indians occasionally burned small areas to trap grasshoppers, which were considered a great delicacy, but the burning was good for the prairies and they returned the next spring, greener than before.

I recall once when, at the urging of innocent but ill-advised friends, I gave momentary consideration to their idea that I should run for a seat in the United States Senate. I can think of no better place for a man with any remaining principles to lose them. I had, for many years, envisioned Congress as a den of moral lepers who owe their souls to those who fill their begging bowls. I did not understand then, nor do I now, how one might be thrown into such a pit without becoming diseased himself.

I had not gotten very far into my cogitation on the matter before I got a call from a young lawyer. Although he was a member of my party, as was his father before him, he and his firm represented some of the major uranium corporations in the state.

"What do you intend to do for the uranium industry?" he asked.

"I've never given that much thought," I confessed. "But as I think about it, I've never liked the uranium industry much. My experience is that we first destroy the prairies to extract the ore, and in the process of mining it and turning the ore into 'yellow cake' we expose the workers to death from cancer." I was on a roll, but not one likely to advance a political career. "After that the product is used to fuel nuclear power plants and to arm nuclear warheads. I should think we could do more social good by growing poppies for the production of opium, which I also oppose."

"But what about the jobs of your friends in Riverton?" he asked. For many years I had practiced law in the little town of Riverton, Wyoming, a prosperous and proud farming community supported by homesteaders who had taken up lands on a federal reclamation project. In the 1960s, uranium was discovered in the Gas Hills area nearby, and the town had boomed, but since then cheaper foreign uranium had flooded the market. "What about the jobs of all those people?" the young lawyer insisted. There was a long silence on the telephone. "Well?" he pushed.

Finally I said, "I don't know how to answer your question. It seems like a conundrum to me. For men to have jobs to support their families we have to put them in those death pits to take part in the destruction of the earth. Let me think about it."

After that I called one of my environmentalist friends and told her of my encounter with the uranium question. "What's the answer?" I asked. "People have to have jobs."

She was both a pragmatic politician and an environmentalist. "I flew over the Gas Hills not so long ago," she said. "I think we were flying at about twenty-five thousand feet. From that altitude what they did to the Gas Hills didn't look too bad."

"Is that your answer?" I asked.

"I don't know any other answer," she said. "People need jobs. We have to let them rape a little."

Rape a little.

Already I was feeling the impotence that every conscientious public servant must feel. I ran, but not for public office. I ran from the dilemma with its equally obnoxious alternatives—that either I threaten the very people I cared for most by refusing to support the industries that provided their jobs, or I lie to them in order to gain their support. Moreover, that in order to tolerate the rape I would have to fly at twenty-five thousand feet over the gaping remains of once-virginal plains did not strike me as a satisfactory solution to our environmental problems.

The answer, of course, is for an enlightened society to change the choices. The answer is to provide jobs for people in industries that do not require us to rape a little. But I had no immediate solutions, and being against rape, a lot or a little, it was easy to see I had no business in politics. It was also easy to see that until we have changed the choices, the earth's freedom, like our own, will remain chiefly irrelevant to the masses of American workers.

But there is another dynamic at work that is destined to do us in. Like my pickup truck, the earth has a limited carrying capacity. Today the earth's population is 5.4 billion people. Already our forests, our oceans, our atmosphere, are strained. Even so the World Bank estimates that by the end of the next century our population will reach about 12.5 billion. Many believe the earth's population will creep even higher, perhaps as high as 14 billion.

Our population continues to rise because, paradoxically, those who can least afford children have the most. To the very poor, children provide their only security in old age, and because the poor practice little or no birth control, they have even more children than their anticipated security demands. At some point the accumulated total of this population explosion, powered by the powerlessness of the poor, will exceed the ability of the earth to carry the load, the consequences of which will be visited upon every living occupant of this planet.

Yet I am heartened when I hear noted thinkers and authors such as Donnella H. Meadows say, "The primary way to deal with the population problem is obvious. It's that short simple word—*share*. Poverty must be ended, once and for all. But how to do that?" Meadows asks. "I don't know in detail. But I do know how to start. The way to start is to look the poor in the face and call them brothers and sisters."

Man is trapped. He is trapped in his symbiotic relationship with both the living and the dead—with both his dependence on nature and his subservience to corporate America. He must preserve the earth lest he destroy himself. Yet he is dependent upon and still serves the most powerful tyrant in the history of the world, a tyrant bent on the destruction of the earth for profit.

We are the new Indians. At the time our native Americans were vanquished, they cried out in impotent rage as their land, their mountains and streams, their great buffalo herds, their beaver and deer and elk, were wrested from them and they themselves were herded onto desolate reservations. Once confined to their reservations they became dependent on the white man for their sustenance, not unlike our confinement today in the megacities where we, too, are dependent on our corporate masters for survival.

The white man gave the Indian trinkets and beads and Christianity and plows and, of course, firewater and disease. We have been provided Bud and Miller and Coors as symbols of happiness, and Marlboros as a symbol of manhood and freedom. We have been sold sickness and death. We have been furnished with every kind and character of machine, with every gadget and thing the mind can concoct, and, to pay for the same, and the interest the banks demand, we have been sentenced to work in places where people ought not to work and to labor for corporate objectives that are contrary to the best interests of the earth and her inhabitants.

We have been magically transformed into a new dual-purpose, double-headed, four-handed mechanism, one more efficient than any heretofore known in the history of the world. One head and two of the hands labor to produce. The other head and two hands insatiably consume the product of our own labor. We are the wonder of wonders. Without us nothing could be produced and without us nothing would be consumed. And, of course, without us there would be no profit for our corporate overlords.

Although he committed no crimes, the Indian was sentenced to work as the white man worked. Smohalla, the great teacher of the Nez Percés, cried out, "My young men shall never work. Men who work cannot dream; and wisdom comes to us in dreams.

"You ask me to plow the ground. Shall I take a knife and tear my mother's breast?

"You ask me to dig for stone. Shall I dig under her skin for her bones? Then when I die I cannot enter her body to be born again.

"You ask me to cut grass and make hay and sell it and be rich like white men. But how dare I cut off my mother's hair?"

We are the new Indians. I remember how my father worked for the railroad, with my mother helping at home. They were able to provide for us. We lived in a small Wyoming town. Like the Indian women who made jerky and pemmican, my mother gardened and canned the vegetables as well as the trout we caught in the streams. Canned, the trout tasted like salmon. The turnips and carrots went into the root cellar for winter.

We had chickens. I remember how we hatched the chicks by the warmth of light bulbs in a box that we set near the furnace. The excess eggs went into "water glass," as it was called, and were preserved for the bitter winter months when the hens stopped laying. We kept a goat in the backyard that provided our milk. It was my job to tend the goat, to see that she got plenty of good green grass that grew along the edges of the alleys. It was also my job to keep her away from wild lettuce and the dandelions that caused her milk to taste bad.

We were Indians in the way we lived. My father hunted. We lived all winter on the deer and elk and antelope he brought home. And we shared it with neighbors who had no hunting fathers. My mother made my winter coat out of the tanned hides of elk and deer, and my mittens out of the lighter skins of antelope.

I remember how my father felt about the great outdoors. Sometimes my mother would scold that we should go to church when instead in the summer we went fishing, and in the fall our family moved to the mountains in our tent to hunt.

"A person can worship God a good deal better out in God's church," the mountains, "than in some man-made stuffy building in town," my father would reply, and I thought he was right.

Yet in other ways I was not Indian. Born in town, in captivity, when I was alone in the mountains I often felt afraid. I remember when my father would take me hunting, and when I was too young to keep up with him as he stayed on the track of a deer in new snow, sometimes he would deposit me in a safe place like the doe leaves her fawn.

"Stay here," he would say, pointing to a group of fallen logs along the trail that provided shelter. "I'll come back for you."

"Don't leave me alone," I'd cry. I was eight or ten. "I'm afraid." I remember looking in every direction. There was nothing civilized in sight—no roads, no houses, no people, only mountain unfolding on mountain. In the silence of the forest there were no sounds except the chatter of a squirrel or the occasional scolding of a jay.

"You're safe here. You're in the mountains," my father would say.

For a child who lived in town, the mountains were wild, but to my father, who was born in the mountains, they were wondrous and safe. He was a part of them.

"The only thing a man needs to be afraid of is other men," my father said. "There aren't any men up here. Bad men are too lazy to come this far." To my father, like the Indian, nature was neither wild nor hostile. Nature was as safe and warm as mother.

After the Second War things changed. Millions of people were forced to the cities in search of work. Farms and small farming communities were abandoned. Like the Indians from whom the people had once taken the land, the people were now forced to give it up, this time to the New King, this time to corporate farming, corporate land developers and to new industries that wrested the land from them.

Where before the Indian needed nothing except what was readily available from the earth, now he was taught that he needed houses and plumbing and automobiles and beer. We too were taught new needs. Our families no longer raised a garden in the backyard and canned our own produce. We bought our food from Safeway. We bought deepfreezes and filled them with frozen products from corporate farming. We no longer picked berries in the fall and ate wild game all winter long. We bought steaks fattened on corn and began to die of obesity and heart attacks. It was no longer lawful to keep a goat tethered in the alley. We bought dairy products produced by corporate farms and marketed by corporate associations, and our coats and mittens were manufactured in foreign countries. Like the Indians imprisoned on the reservation, we soon forgot how to live on the earth.

Our fathers were no longer able to earn the family's living. We therefore sent our mothers out of the home to work to pay for the trinkets and the gadgets, the second automobile and the automatic washing machine and dryer and television set and telephones, the boats and campers and on and on. In the meantime we sent our children to day care so that, in the end, we traded our mothers for the gadgetry we had been trained to covet.

As their land was taken from them, the Indians cried out in deep sorrow. We hear the same cries now from our farmers who have lost their farms to banks, from our ranchers who have had to cut up their holdings into small ranchettes and sell them to eastern moneyed men who come in the summer, don their cowboy hats and their spurs, and ride a fancy purebred horse in the Fourth of July parade. We hear the same Indian cry from those left behind in deserted villages when their neighbors have been shipped off to the cities. We hear the same cry from the small businessmen in the towns who have been systematically replaced by nonresident corporate franchises.

Indeed, we are the new Indians. Entrapped in our concrete reservations, indentured to our corporate masters, impoverished of our land, separated from the earth, and at last placed at odds with nature herself, many no longer see the issue of freedom as relevant. For them the ring of the liberty bell has long ago been silenced. And, having lost our connection with our mother earth, we have lost our connection with ourselves.

I think again of my childhood. I am sitting alone on the log in the wilderness waiting for my father to return. I am lost. I do not know where our camp lies nor how far. I am afraid. The sun is growing low over the horizon. The cold bite of evening begins to settle in. I wiggle my toes against my boot soles to keep them warm. New shivers begin to make their way along my ribs. I feel panic.

Then I see my father coming. He has a great smile on his face. He has been all day on the trail of a deer and there is fresh blood on his hands, which is good news, for he has been successful. I shout with joy, "Daddy, Daddy!"

"Well, I see you are just fine," he says as if he had been gone for only minutes.

"I was afraid something had happened to you and that you wouldn't come back."

"Well, I told you, there's nothing to be afraid of here. And I was right, wasn't I?" He smiles at me and waits for my answer.

# 8

# T R E E   H U G G E R

*The*

*Tyranny*

*of*

*Viewpoint*

*I have lived alone for important parts of my life. And I* have often felt lonely even though I was surrounded by a host of living things. My loneliness was, as always, born of my separation from myself, and, therefore, from all other living things as well. I remember. The summer was gone, the robins had gone, and the shy, slate-colored Juncos had gathered and gone. The blue harebell had dried and twisted toward the earth, and the parachute seeds of the dandelions in the meadow had long ago blown away. Their stems stood straight and stiff, and the leaves of the elk thistle were like curled, brown memories. I felt the sharp teeth of loneliness gnawing at my heart. I tried to comfort myself with reason. But reason is not often comforting.

We are all, all alone, I reasoned. Alone we struggle from the womb. Alone we float down the inescapable river of life. Alone we face the falls, the horrible, doomful falls. Alone we wheeze out our last mortal gasp. I looked out the window at the slender aspen tree. Then something compelled me to get up and walk out to it. Suddenly I wanted to talk to the tree.

To talk to a tree—that is strange, is it not? Yet no one thinks it odd for man to speak to something he cannot see or touch, something he calls "God." No one thinks it bizarre that we listen and are impelled into strange actions, such as buying a certain soft drink because an electronic image we cannot touch says the drink contains the magical "Uh-huh." Yet if we were to shake hands with a tree, with something real, something with its roots in the ground, something that lives, that grows, that rustles in the wind, something in which living birds build nests and hatch their young—if we were to touch a tree and to speak to it, we might be considered very peculiar indeed. The tyranny of viewpoint, most often not our own, constricts us as surely as a horse's hobbles.

The Indian thought it ordinary to communicate with animals and plants and trees. Tatanga Mani, or Walking Buffalo, of the Stony Indians of Canada, said, "Did you know that trees talk? Well, they do. They talk to each other and they'll talk to you if you listen. Trouble is, white people don't listen. They never learned to listen to the Indians so I don't suppose they'll listen to other voices in nature. But I have learned a lot from trees; sometimes about the weather, sometimes about animals, sometimes about the Great Spirit."

I'm sure that my neighbors would have thought me quite daft had they seen me talking to this aspen. But I was alone, and alone one has the right, by reason of his aloneness, to do as he pleases. Alone, one is free, or ought to be. And so, I thought, I shall see how it is to speak to a tree. I looked around to make sure. No one was within miles of my cabin. No one was watching. No one would hear me. And yet I had a difficult time bringing myself to do this simple, harmless thing. I confess, I am the kind who has never mustered the courage to write on a toilet wall. I suppose, subconsciously, I think God is watching. I also hear my dear dead mother's admonition, "Fools' names and fools' faces are always found in public places." Maybe my mother would be watching.

We are as free as the fences we have constructed around our minds' permit. Indeed, as we perceive it, insanity may be simply the elimination of all of the mind's fences. We know that trees do not talk. Yet I might conclude that my neighbors also do not talk. I have never heard them speak, but that is because I have never spoken to them. If I judged the ability of the human race to communicate based on my experience with my neighbors, I should likely conclude that the species is mute. In the same way, since I have never spoken to a tree, how could I possibly expect a tree to speak to me? Still, this was, indeed, strange behavior, this tree talking, and I decided I would not mention this to my friends and family, who already thought me strange enough.

I looked around once more to make sure no one was watching. Then suddenly I reached out and grasped the lowest limb of the tree, like one shaking hands. "Tree," to my horror I heard myself saying out loud, "I just dropped over to say hello." It was easy. There was no parting of the clouds, no voice descending upon me, saying, "Now you have finally done it! I have patiently endured your faithless pronouncements against me, and against my faithful, but talking to trees—this is finally too much!"

"Tree," I said, "I've seen you almost every day out my cabin window, and often admired you, but for some reason I've never stopped over. People are like that, you know." The tree said nothing back, but I had a sense that somehow my words were being soaked up. I've been with people many times and said things that never were soaked up, things that were important to me, but that, when I offered them to others, just sort of lay there in a puddle.

"You're lucky to have your friends with you all the

time," I said to the tree, "and your kids and your family. Got your roots all tangled up together and your capillaries all entwined, and it's cheek to cheek with those who are closest to you all summer long. And when the wind blows, your leaves caress each other. Must be quite something to have ten thousand leaves to feel with."

I looked up. The tree's leaves had already fallen. After a minute I just came out with it. "I felt lonely today. That's why I'm out here speaking to you," I said, and the tears came to my eyes, and I didn't feel ashamed crying in front of a tree, although I have always felt shame in crying in front of people. "Thanks for listening to me," I said. "That's what friends are for," and I gave the tree a loving pat.

But the tree didn't answer.

"I don't think people understand me," I said.

Still the tree didn't answer. But in the utter silence of the aspen grove I heard a clear response. We must each find our own answers—both the tree and I. That is freedom. A tree's answers would not do for me. It moves with the wind, and with the seasons. Its feet are in the soil. It is part of the earth. Its wisdom is, perhaps, too great to be imparted to the likes of me. Yet somehow I felt very wise after having listened to the tree.

"Thank you, tree." I said. "It helps a lot to have a true friend to talk to."

Then before I left, I asked the tree the *one* question of all questions:

"Tree"—I waited until I knew I must have its attention—"what is the meaning of life?" Again there was a long silence. "Speak up, dear friend. Oh, how I need to know!"

Nothing.

"Please!"

Nothing.

And then, suddenly I knew the answer (although I have since forgotten it) and I threw my arms around the tree, and that's how I became a tree hugger.

*Ideas, not our own, entrap us, govern us, enslave. We harbor,* for instance, the idea that we should eat cereal for breakfast and chile for lunch, not vice versa, although the body tolerates a switching of the fare quite satisfactorily. We think it all right to eat pigs but not dogs, although both are eaten with relish in China, and a pig is as intelligent, as feeling, as capable of being loyal and loving as any poodle. We think it wrong to kill wild animals for their pelts but we suffer no hesitation whatever in killing little soft-eyed calves to eat and from which to make our gloves and shoes. We maintain "animal shelters" for stray dogs and cats while some of our own species starve and die on the streets. We say, poetically, that only God can make a tree and then destroy whole forests to make toilet paper.

Rights—the rights of man as well as the rights of all other living things—are dictated by ideas, by viewpoints we accept as truth but most of which cannot survive the first cursory inspection. With that in mind it might be permissible as well as amusing to reexamine the wholly irrational idea that things in nature possess no rights of their own. We recall it was the venerable Justice William O. Douglas of the United States Supreme Court who argued, vainly, that trees have standing to bring suit. Were such a case to actually come before a Wyoming court, I can envision the argument proceeding approximately like this:

"Trees have standing? What do you mean, Counsel, that trees have standing?" the judge shouted.

His name was Robert P. Hammond. People called him "R.P." Some who had experienced his unpredictable blasts of intemperance had added an *I* between his initials.

"Well, let us see if we can work through this thing logically. 'Reason is the life of the law,' somebody said."

"Lord Coke said it, Your Honor," I offered.

"That sounds reasonable," Judge Hammond said. "Lord Coke was always coming off with dicta like that so people could chisel his words above courthouse doors. So why, Counsel, shouldn't the law protect trees?" he asked Richard Hallmark Benyon, of Stutts, Slister, Benyon, Benyon, and Benyon. It was one of those megafirms of five hundred lawyers that charges four or five hundred dollars an hour for its services to America's great business organizations and it touted three generations of Benyons in its name, none of whom would have been remembered otherwise.

"Trees are not *sui juris!*" Benyon cried, pounding his fist on the table.

"*Sui juris?* Indeed!" the judge said. "Can you buy it at the health-food store?"

"Let us not be facetious, Your Honor," Benyon replied. "Obviously one must be a member of the *human* species to be *sui juris.*"

"The law protects nonpeople too," I said. "Corporations are *sui juris* and corporations aren't members of the human species."

"That is patently false!" Benyon shouted.

"Please don't shout!" Judge Hammond shouted. "We may frighten Reason right out of this courtroom. Reason is fragile and cannot bear much shouting."

"Corporations are *not* made up of people," I whispered. "People *work* for corporations and *slave* for corporations and even *die* for corporations, but corporations are *not* people." It was my standard argument. "Corporations are not alive. You can't even see a corporation."

"Mr. Benyon, have you ever seen a corporation?" the judge asked.

"That's ridiculous. Of course I've seen a corporation."

"Tell me, what did the corporation that you saw look like?"

"Well, Your Honor, if facetiousness runs both ways,

let me say that Chrysler looked like Lee Iacocca and General Electric looked like Ronald Reagan."

"But *was* General Electric Ronald Reagan? Reason, gentlemen! Reason! If a corporation is merely an *it,* as Mr. Spence insists, and if this pencil is an *it,* then does *it* not follow that a corporation is like a pencil?"

Benyon turned away in disgust. "This has gone far enough."

"A corporation is less than a pencil," I said, "you can *see* a pencil."

"You mean to say that General Electric is less than a pencil?" Judge Hammond whispered, raising both eyebrows.

"You can't make any logic whatever of corporations," I said. "Yet they own everything—even our congressmen and presidents."

"Let's not get into politics!" Benyon shouted again. "This is a court of law."

"They pass our laws," I continued. "They own the media. Less-than-nothings control *everything.* It is quite crazy, I should say, Your Honor."

"Why, logically, I do believe you're right, Spence. Wouldn't you agree, Benyon?"

"Corporations are not less-than-nothings. Corporations are *everything!* We couldn't exist without corporations!" Benyon was shouting again. "Everything worth doing is done *by* corporations, *through* corporations, and *for* corporations. When we get up in the morning, we brush our teeth with toothpaste manufactured by a corporation, and it's a corporation that manufactures the television we watch while eating our breakfast cereal, which is also manufactured by a corporation. We drive to work in a car built by a corporation, and sleep every night on a bed manufactured by a corporation. We spend our lives working for corporations, and . . . " He ran out of breath.

"And we are buried in a casket with a jumbo Simmons Beautyrest mattress sold by a corporation," I added.

"Exactly!" Benyon shouted back. "For once we see eye to eye on something, Spence. We are born in a corporate hospital and buried by a corporate mortuary. America is one big corporation!"

"*Shh,*" Judge Hammond cautioned again. "You mean to tell me that America is just a big conglomeration of corporations like a bunch of fish eggs stuck together lying on the bottom of the creek?" The judge was an angler of local fame.

"You could say that," Benyon said. "However, with all due respect, I'm not too sure there isn't a better metaphor. America is more like a . . . "

"Like a beautiful forest made up of many beautiful trees?" I suggested.

"That's more like it!" Benyon agreed.

"Now we are getting somewhere," the judge said. "Does each tree in this forest have standing?"

"Every tree in the corporate forest has standing," Benyon said. "The courts have given corporations standing since *Marbury v. Madison.*"

"That *is* strange," the judge whispered, gazing up at the ceiling.

"Why, Your Honor?" Benyon asked, looking perplexed.

"That nonliving trees, those fictional trees you call corporations, should have standing, but *living* trees should not. Don't you find that rather anomalous, Mr. Benyon?"

"We are dealing with mere metaphor, Your Honor, mere fiction."

"Yes, of course," Judge Hammond said. "But corporations are fictions too—mere legal fictions. Therefore, does it not follow that we give a mere fiction more rights than we give a real, living, growing tree?"

"As you know, Your Honor, logic can take one to strange places."

"Yes, Mr. Benyon, logic *can* take one to strange places." The judge gazed up at the oak beams overhead. "That which cannot be seen has rights—but a real living tree, which everyone can see, does not! A legal fiction has the same rights as you and I, but that which is alive does not! Yes, Mr. Benyon, logic does take us to very strange places. Perhaps we should no longer trust logic. Things either do or do not have rights. What do you say to that?"

By now Benyon was strutting back and forth in front of the bench, anticipating his victory, his thumbs tucked into his vest pockets. "But what are *things?*" the judge asked.

"Things are things and need no definition," Benyon hastily replied.

"I say things *do* need definition," the judge said. "The Supreme Court of the United States decreed that the American slave was a *thing,* and as such he could be bought and sold like any other thing. No, Benyon. What is or is not a thing is what we declare a thing to be."

"Well, inanimate things have no rights," Benyon said. "We can surely agree on that. Do you see that little tassel on my shoe, Your Honor?"

"Those shoes drive me crazy," the judge said. "I've been watching those silly little doodaddies on attorneys' shoes for years."

"That doodaddy, as you call it, has no rights because that doodaddy is a *thing.*"

"You've convinced me," the judge said. "Things have no rights. And if a living forest is merely a thing, then the forest has no standing."

"Precisely!" Benyon said. "So I take it you grant my motion to dismiss the alleged 'living forest' out of this lawsuit."

Then the judge stared down at Benyon. "What is the source of our rights, Benyon?"

"The law, of course."

"Thank you, Benyon. And so the black slave, a thing, had no rights merely because the law said he had none. And when the slaves were freed and blacks were given equal rights, that occurred because, again, the law simply said so, right?"

"Right."

"So whether something is a *thing* depends on what the law says, and nothing more."

"Perhaps," Benyon said, not liking the direction the judge's logic was taking.

"Corporations—less than things—have rights because the law gives them rights, right?"

Benyon nodded skeptically.

"And, therefore, Mr. Benyon, if the law can declare that fictions have rights, does it not follow that the party called the 'living forest' can also have rights? All I have to do is to declare their rights, right?"

Benyon was silent. And for a long time the judge was silent too. Finally he spoke, "Mr. Benyon, I hereby declare that the living forest has standing in this court and may sue your client for its damages."

"Trees and squirrels and . . . and spiders and snakes can sue?" Benyon was dumbfounded. "Have you lost your mind?"

"I certainly have," Judge Hammond said. "Good riddance."

"I object," I said.

"*You* object, Spence?" Judge Hammond asked, astounded. "Don't you understand? I've just held *for* you."

"I disagree with the basis of your holding, Your Honor, with all due respect. I mean, sir, didn't you just hold that things, whether they were things or less-than-things, obtained their rights through the law?"

"Yes, of course, Spence. All rights are derived from the law."

"Men make the law?" I asked.

"And *women*," the judge, correct in his politics, hastened to add. "Yes, of course man- and womankind, let us say, personkind, makes the law. What could possibly be your objection, Spence?"

"I object to such, ah—what shall I call it?"

"Call it what you want," Judge Hammond said. "This is a free country."

"Well, thank you, sir. In that case, I will call it a stupid and arrogant holding."

"Are you calling this court stupid *and* arrogant?"

"Yes, sir, but with all due respect, sir, and only with your permission."

"I find you in contempt of court, Spence."

"Well, Your Honor, since I'm in contempt of court, might I ask you a question?"

"Of course, Spence. Ask away. You are free to speak. I am free to find you in contempt. That seems fair, doesn't it?"

"Yes, it does, Your Honor. With that in mind, may I ask, who gave man the right to bestow these rights?"

"Spence, man's right to bestow rights on his fellow man came from God, and God is not arrogant or stupid. Don't forget, we judges do God's work."

"Well, sir, I believe that trees and rocks and dandelions and creeks and creatures, including the two-toothed snail and all the other creatures and mountains and prairies and living forests—all have rights *on their own*. By reason of their *being*, they have rights. Man does not *give* rights. He only takes them away."

"Now that's an interesting idea, Spence!"

"It *is* interesting if you think about it, sir. If a thug goes into a little grocery store and holds his gun to the head of the owner, would you say that the store owner's rights are *derived* from the thug?"

"What are you driving at, Spence? We haven't got all day. My rear end, as it were, is getting tired."

"With all due respect, Your Honor, I'm trying to say that although the store owner's right to live may well depend upon what the thug does with his gun, nevertheless, the store owner had a right to live *before* the thug came into his store."

"Are you calling me a thug, Spence?"

"Of course not, Your Honor. But with all due respect, Your Honor, I'm merely attempting to prevent you from acting like one. I don't believe you can point your judicial gun and bestow rights as you please.

Those trees had rights *to begin with*. Some of the trees Mr. Benyon's client has already destroyed were full-grown trees before you were born, Your Honor."

"So what, Spence? You are making the seat of the judiciary, shall we call it, very tired." He lifted himself off his chair and settled in again.

"Well, Your Honor, if those trees were in existence *before* you were born, and if they now have rights, as you say they do, doesn't it follow that they had such rights all along? Otherwise trees would never have rights until *you* were born and *you* grew up and *you* took the bench and *you* just happened to bestow such rights on them. Without *you*, trees would be without rights. That would be arrogant and stupid, wouldn't you say, with all due respect, Your Honor?"

"Spence, you're right! My genius is not in right thinking but in *recognizing* right thinking. Your logic is irrefutable and infallible, Spence. Reason is, indeed, the life of the law."

"It is only fair to warn you, Your Honor, that I am probably insane. I speak to trees."

"So what, Spence? Many great men were insane. Insanity is *it!*" Judge Hammond shouted. "Nietzsche was insane. Van Gogh was insane. Poe was insane. But were they *wrong?* I hold that you are *right*, Spence. I hold that the grocer did have rights before the thug put the gun to his head. I therefore find that the living forest had rights *ab initio*."

"*Ab* who?" Benyon demanded.

"From the beginning, counsel! The living forest has had rights from the beginning. Isn't that so, Spence?"

"Well, yes, sir, I believe so, Your Honor. It seems to me that rights are derived from *being*."

"Then jelly beans have rights," Benyon said sarcastically.

"And you have rights," Judge Hammond responded. "You have the right to take my decision to the court of appeals. By the way, Spence, how much will you be asking the jury for?"

"Well, sir, let me put it this way: The world's forests are the home of half of the ten billion species that live on the face of the earth. They provide us with food and much of our medicine; they cool the earth by absorbing carbon dioxide and provide us with the very oxygen we breathe. The forests are the earth's lungs. Yet, sir, our forests are being destroyed at the rate of fifty million acres or more a year. Less than a few lifetimes remain before the forests of the earth are wiped out and that, sir, could bring life as we know it to an end. My problem is, sir, that I don't know how to measure what is beautiful and alive in terms of money, which is quite dead."

"Yes," Judge Hammond said. "Well, we shall see what the morrow brings. The jury will be excused until nine A.M. In the meantime will the bailiff please come forward."

The bailiff, a very old man, toddled toward the bench.

"You are ordered to take Mr. Spence into your custody, Mr. Bailiff, and to incarcerate him in the county jail until he has purged himself of his contempt for this court."

"But, Your Honor, I thought you said I was right," I protested.

"That you are right does not mean you were not contemptuous of this court. Remember that Galileo was right, too. But he was found in contempt of the church."

"But, Your Honor, does that mean that I have to stay in jail for four hundred years until I am finally absolved?"

"We shall see what the morrow brings," the judge said again. "In the meantime, Mr. Bailiff, have no fear of Mr. Spence. He is quite harmless. He is one of those tree huggers, you know. Be careful he does not confuse your leg for a stump."

# Eve's Return to the Garden

## *The*

## *Tyranny*

## *of*

## *Maleness*

*I do not like it when I hear an employer say, "I let my workers* speak their minds." He must also claim the right to deny his workers free speech. Who endows any person with such rights?

I do not like it when I hear an environmentalist say, "I think we should save the spotted owl." That person must also claim the right to determine the fate of all creatures. By what right does he play God over forests or owls?

I do not like it when I hear a man say, "I think women should have equal rights." He must believe that, if he chose, women would have no rights at all. Who gave that man such power?

I do not like it when I hear a husband magnanimously say, "I let my wife do what she wants." He must mean that he could, if he chose, withhold her freedom, which means, of course, that she was not free in the first place.

How does man justify such arrogance? How did he

become endowed with the right to dominate, to control, to destroy, to tamper with, to pollute, to kill, to maim, and to enslave? How does his control extend to every creature, to every bud and tree, indeed, to every living thing—to the soil, the rivers, the seas, the sky, the whole earth, my great God almighty, the universe itself?

When I speak of man, I speak of *civilized* man. But one should never believe adjectives. Adjectives, especially as used by those who want our money or our vote, explain not how things are but how things are not. If you see a sign on a motel proclaiming there are "modern rooms" within, you know the hotel is likely a flophouse. If you are told by a politician that he is "kinder and gentler," you know he possesses the heart of a San Quentin guard else he would have no need to advertise otherwise. If we are told we are equal, we are usually enslaved. If we are told we are free, we usually owe our souls to the company store. And when we speak of *civilized* man we do not describe a species that is polite or refined or courteous or one that reflects good breeding, but a monstrously insensitive, aggressive creature bent on destroying himself and all that exists on earth. The only *civilized* man was savage man who, like the squirrel, lived in harmony with the other creatures of the earth with remarkable success for over two million years.

The Bible confirms the widely accepted myth that God gave man the right to dominate the earth and all its creatures. But he who gives power must also have the power to take it away. I dare say that if God were as alert as the drunken owner of a flophouse he would have kicked man out of the premises long ago. He would have kicked him out for having chopped holes in the walls and broken the mirrors, for having killed the manager's dog and cat, for having eaten his canary, for having defecated in the lobby, brawled in the coffee shop, for having sold the silverware, and finally for having set fire to the place.

If, in the history of the universe, "civilized man" is to be remembered, he will be recalled not as a creature of superior intellect, for his mind has been employed principally in the destruction of the earth, not as a creature of superior grace, for he has willingly destroyed everything that he touches, not for his tender sensibilities, for over the eons he has demonstrated the sensitivity of a warthog in the lilies. He will be remembered, instead, as the creature of perfect arrogance.

The Indian, the savage, understood a simple truth. Man does not own the earth. Indeed, the idea of ownership is as estranged from truth as is the notion that one man can own the soul of another. Upon being asked for his signature on a treaty with the United States, a chief of the Northern Blackfeet said, "The land was put here for us by the Great Spirit and we cannot sell it because it does not belong to us." Instead, the Indian belonged to the land. In our arrogance we often get things backwards.

The arrogance of man is derived from his frightful awareness of his temporal condition. Knowing that he will die, and that he must die alone, he attempts to grasp eternal life by controlling, by possessing, even by killing, all that surrounds him. Fearful of his fate after having squandered his few miserable years on earth, man, afraid and alone, pretends he is God. For God lives forever.

Arrogance is the offspring of terror. If man were a flower and could communicate with butterflies, if he were only a lowly mole and could speak to worms, perhaps he would not feel so alone, so vulnerable, so alienated. Among the creatures, man is able to speak only to himself. Yet if he could hear the other creatures, perhaps he could acquire small insights into their wisdom. Perhaps he would not clutch so compulsively at anything and everything. Perhaps he would no longer be so afraid. It is as if man, maddened by fear, has decreed that if he must die, then the earth and all that live upon it must also.

In the same way, and out of the same inexhaustible fund of terror, man, with but one weapon to brandish against his terror, namely his superior power over his mate, seeks to dominate her. The idea is simple. If he can control the possessor of the womb from which he was expelled, if he can dominate the source of his life, he can, somehow, also dominate death.

Yet in recent times a new arrogance has become the new tyranny of maleness. I say it is a new tyranny because it is founded in the ultimate arrogance of maleness, the proclamation of males in that high-pitched sound, as if it were being choked from them, that women *should* be free. The proclamation itself exposes the arrogance, for men are not the source of women's freedom. Even the less offensive statement, "Women have the same rights as we," smacks of the same, for this, too, is the male proclamation. How do men proclaim their friends, their neighbors, free or enslaved? Only tyrants proclaim whole peoples free or enslaved. Legitimately, men can only proclaim their own freedom. The correct statement concerning women's equality is, in fact, no statement at all. The correct statement is the continuous and determined acts of men that buttress respect for women and demonstrate their equality.

Sadly, women themselves have readily accepted the paradigm that puts maleness at the top of a totem pole with women anguishing in the deep under-shade. Consequently women see men as their enemy, men who exclusively and wrongfully occupy the top of the totem, men as the dominant sex, men as the tyrannical force that withholds their freedom, men as the nucleus of a system that enslaves them. And they also see that if they are to be free, they must petition men for their freedom or else, by war of one kind or another, turn the tables of domination. I say the paradigm is irrelevant, that men at the top of a totem are merely men at the top of a totem. It is *their* totem. And, judging from their successes in maintaining peace, administering justice, and alleviating suffering and hunger, I should think that no thoughtful woman, or anyone else for that matter, would seek to share their place of power. To say that men are irrelevant to women's freedom is not, however, to say that men do not control. It is to say that men have no right to control and that they are not the wellspring of women's rights. Women were born with their rights. As the saying goes, they were "born free."

Man's dominance is pathological. His control is compulsive and ill. Adopting for the sake of argument the paradigm that woman is imprisoned on the earth with her wearisomely ill cell mate, man, no thoughtful woman would likely petition him for her freedom. Women cannot be free until they, not men, declare themselves free. They cannot be free until they disengage from the struggle with those who hold illegitimate power over them, until they recognize maleness as utterly irrelevant to their rights. The struggle is against the notion that men are the rootstock of both women's freedom and their servitude. The struggle is to focus the battle so that women may recognize that women, and women alone, are the source of their rights, here and hereafter.

But in a complex world where men control the jobs, the wages, the politics, the religious institutions, where men, by reason of their pathology, clutch and control like children with a death grip around their mothers' legs, the correct action for women is often difficult to visualize. At the workplace, where women compete with men for the same jobs but for lesser wages, the hue and cry is, understandably, "Equal pay for equal work." The reaction is to attack the male who receives the better dollar for the identical job. But often it is not the male worker who deprives his female counterpart of equality. It is their mutual corporate oppressor. And although the corporate employer, too, is male-dominated, the motivating force is not to discriminate against women because they are women, but to exploit the worker, male or female, for the profit of the corporation.

I have never seen a case in which a corporation dominated by women gives women better rights than men. The issue is most often not sex but money. The issue is not women's rights as opposed to men's rights, but profit. If corporate America thought it could make more by giving men less and women more, it would do so. Instead, the game is to exploit any who are exploitable. Women, often less organized, less represented, less entrenched with less history in the male-dominated workplace, and who often suffer greater needs and exist in more desperate straits, are the easier target.

That men dominate in politics is merely a historical extension of men wielding their superior physical strength to wrest power. Today our national leaders, nearly all male, are chosen from the socially more powerful males of our culture, where leadership is still usurped by power, under the mistaken assumption that power and wisdom, power and competence, power and morality, are somehow equivalent. Perhaps more than any other phenomenon, male domination of our public offices, although waning, illustrates how power is born of power; that is, because men have usurped power over the eons by use of physical force, the assumption is that men, being more powerful physically, socially, and economically, are therefore also more qualified to lead. Women's equality will come when such myths are finally exposed.

The well-balanced, intelligent, fully integrated male rarely seeks power. Power is an unfortunate palliative for the insecure, and in our male-dominated culture insecurity is a sex-related illness. To permit power-hungry males to rule, whether through the so-called democratic processes or by use of stealth or force, is like turning a pyromaniac loose in a match factory with a large can of gasoline.

When we find tyrants we most often find men who fill in the gaps and holes in their personality with power. Tyrants use power like putty to fill in for knowledge, for understanding, for intelligence, for patience, for insight, for sensitivity. Eventually we mistakenly come to see power as wisdom. Yet the most powerful are often the most obtuse, as evidenced by the fact that the world, suffering through its tragic history of war, genocide, starvation, ignorance, and misery, has been under the nearly exclusive domination of men from the onset of civilization. It would be a risk-free experiment were women to take over the sole leadership of the world for the next ten thousand years, considering the miserable record men have established as leaders throughout our dismal history.

At times when benevolence overcomes judgment, I find myself arguing that the entire problem is merely chemical. Testosterone, that fiendish substance that indiscriminately, cruelly ravishes the bodies of boys and men, compels the male of the species to commit every variety of monstrous act from rape to nuclear warfare. Such diabolical acts, whether committed by the penis of the flesh or the larger penis of intercontinental missiles, mimic each other. Both are attacks against the female, one against woman, the other against mother earth.

I have recently learned of a little-noticed study scientists at a well-known and highly respected university performed on wiggly-tailed beagle puppies. At six months of age the puppies were injected with massive doses of testosterone. The report recited its conclusion in material part as follows: "Most of these juveniles, unremarkable prior to the injection of twenty mg. of *testosterone enanthate* daily, began emitting weird, rhythmic yappings similar to the 'hard rock' favored by American youth on MTV. Seven were killed in fights in which the victims were literally ripped to pieces. Ninety-seven percent evidenced bizarre sexual behavior, mounting any handy object—a feeding dish, a bone, even each other." Then to my astonishment the article concluded as follows: "Hip baths administered in ice water proved the most effective means of controlling this aberrant conduct." A footnote admitted that the university researchers adopted the hip-bath treatment from the 1931 edition of the *Official Manual of the Boy Scouts of America.*

Although the human males' evil may have been chemically induced, it was also the product of culture. Women's domination by men began with the birth of civilization, with man's departure from nature. As man took up agriculture and established himself in villages instead of wandering and gathering, as he domesticated animals instead of hunting them, indeed, as he separated himself from nature, man began to see himself at odds with the earth. Such early isolationism created the forces of "them and me"—man against the earth, man's village against other villages, man's territory against other territories, man against other men, and, of course, man against woman. As man became fixed in village and field and abdicated his place in the natural order, his separation created for him a new and wholly defective vista of the world.

Disassociated from the natural whole, and estranged from his mother earth, man, once free and easy, became paranoid and delusional. Where once he saw himself as part of the earth, now he saw the earth, his mother, and all her inhabitants as dangerous and hostile. By his separation from nature, he was also separated from other members of his species with whom he now competed for food, for shelter, for territory, for women, and for power.

Where once man enjoyed a perfect wisdom because, as part of nature, he shared nature's perfect knowledge and abided by her laws, now, ignorant and foolish and panicked, he did as ignorant and foolish men do when panicked—he struck out against all that lived, bringing war and starvation, suffering and death, not only to his own species but also to every other species and every other living thing on earth. Yet give man credit where due. He treated all living things equally, that is to say, he as readily destroyed members of his own species as any other. He as readily imposed his injustices on his wives and his children and his weaker neighbors as he did on his mother earth.

His overriding obsession was to dominate woman, for she possessed certain mystical powers man associated with mother earth who, willy-nilly, exerted her devastating power over him. Woman, like the earth, possessed the power to produce life, to produce sustenance for life from her body, the power to give or withhold tenderness, to give joy or to torment. Woman, like the earth, possessed the power to wield the unfathomable power of mothers over sons, of women over husbands, and to the extent that all such power was feminine and was at odds with man, all who possessed such power, the earth and woman alike, were man's enemies. Indeed, man was surrounded by his enemies.

Now possessed by his herds and his fields, man was no longer able to move with the storms and the change of the seasons. He was no longer able to ebb and flow in harmony with the earth. In abject terror, and alone and at odds with the whole from which he was separated, man now created God. And the bargain he struck with God was, indeed, an unholy one, one that far surpassed the evil of Eve when she allegedly cavorted with a beguiling snake and ate of the apple, for man surrendered to God all his power.

In exchange for man's enslavement to God, man was reassured that, so long as God was pleased (and why shouldn't God be pleased, for after all it was man who created God), man would be permitted to dominate his enemies, the earth and all that lived upon the earth, including, of course, woman. Where once man was all-powerful because as a part of nature he moved with nature's irresistible forces, now, separated and having delivered his power to God, he could only pray to God to return to him that which he had given up to God in the first place.

We are told that God made woman from man's rib, symbolizing, of course, her subservience and inferiority to man. The early ecclesiastical scholars put it thus:

> And it should be noted that there was a defect in the formation of the first woman, since she was formed from a bent rib, that is, a rib of the breast which is bent as it were in a contrary direction to a man. And since through this defect she is an imperfect animal, she always deceives.

As the forces of nature were hurled against man, he saw his misery not as a consequence of his separation but, instead, as the curse of his displeased God. Since man, in his infinite arrogance, found himself without fault, he was left no alternative but to blame God's displeasure on women. In 1484, the venerable Bull of Pope Innocent VIII authorized that inquisitions be undertaken by Henry Kramer and James Sprenger, respected professors of theology, and for good cause. The Bull (perhaps the origin of the slang meaning "nonsense") read, in part, as follows:

> It has, indeed lately come to our ears . . . that many persons of both sexes, unmindful of their own salvation and straying from the Catholic Faith, have abandoned themselves to devils, incubi and succubi, and by their incantations, spells, conjurations, and other accursed charms and crafts, enormities and horrid offences, have slain infants yet in the mother's womb, as also the offspring of cattle, have blasted the produce of the earth, the grapes of the vine, the fruits of trees, nay, men and women, beasts of burthen, herd-beasts, as well as animals of other kinds . . . they hinder men from performing the sexual act and women from conceiving, whence husbands cannot know their wives nor wives receive their

husbands . . . they do not shrink from committing and perpetrating the foulest abominations and filthiest excesses to the deadly peril of their own souls, whereby they outrage the Divine Majesty and are a cause of scandal and danger to very many.

Nothing more eloquently exemplifies the first tenet of Christianity, namely forgiveness, than the fact that its followers have through the centuries been able to forgive the unrelenting and egregious sins of the Church. The offenses most often charged by the Inquisitors were heresy and witchcraft. Scholars believe as many as a million women were burned alive as witches. A part of our own heritage not usually recalled in our Fourth of July speeches includes hanging, as witches, the innocent, good wives of Salem in 1692.

When man was a part of the earth he did not fear it, for as part of the earth he could never be destroyed. Without fear man had no cause to destroy. Without fear man had no reason to be arrogant. Without fear man had no reason to dominate woman. As part of the earth man was, indeed, eternal to the same extent that the earth was eternal. Man's ejection from the Garden of Eden records in mythology the tragedy of his separation. By tasting the fruit of the tree of knowledge, he became aware of his alienation from nature, or to put it otherwise, he became cognizant of his mortality.

Terrorized by death and drowning in fear, mortal man began his frenzied quest to wield authority. His attempt to control the earth was his defense. His wars against other members of his species were his defense. His exercise of physical power over women was his defense. At last, his unmitigated arrogance was his piteous defense.

One ought not pass this juncture without acknowledging that man, despite the Christian admonition to "love thy enemies," indeed, hated his enemies. He has hated the earth from the day he was ejected from the garden, as is evidenced by his unremitting poisoning of the rivers, his pollution of the oceans, his fouling of the air, his destruction of the forests, and his rupturing of the earth's tender skin, the ozone. He has hated, not loved, mankind, as is evidenced by the infinite atrocities he has committed against his own. He has hated, not loved, woman, as evidenced by a history of shameless depredations he has committed against her.

Even by the earliest biblical times, a woman, servile to her father, entered a bitter dominance under her husband. Woman had no access to power; she could own no property. If, when married, she was not a virgin, she could be stoned. Adultery, defined as sex by a married woman with a man not her husband, was punishable by death. If a woman was raped, the offender had to pay the bride-price to the father and was required to marry the victim, who could not divorce him. Divorce was the prerogative only of men.

As we have seen, by the time of the Inquisition men were so ravished by fear and maddened by their alienation that they sought to lay their total afflictions at the feet of their wives, their mothers, their daughters, indeed, any female who dared lift up her head. Had not a wicked woman, the original woman, seduced man out of the garden? By the late fifteenth century, the *Malleus Maleficarum,* next to the Bible the most widely disseminated and revered book of the time, the manual of the Inquisition, summed up the case against women:

> Now the wickedness of women is spoken of in Ecclesiastes 25: There is no head above the head of a serpent: and there is no wrath above the wrath of a woman. I had rather dwell with a lion and a dragon than to keep house with a wicked woman. . . . All wickedness is but little to the wickedness of a woman. Wherefore S. John Chrysostom says on the test, It is not good to marry (Matthew 19): What else is woman but a foe to

friendship, an unescapable punishment, a necessary evil, a natural temptation, a desirable calamity, a domestic danger, a delectable detriment, an evil of nature, painted with fair colours! Therefore if it be a sin to divorce her when she ought to be kept, it is indeed a necessary torture; for either we commit adultery by divorcing her, or we must endure daily strife. Cicero in his second book of *The Rhetorics* says: The many lusts of men lead them into one sin, but the one lust of woman leads them into all sins; for the root of all woman's vices is avarice. And Seneca says in his *Tragedies:* A woman either loves or hates; there is no third grade. And the tears of a woman are a deception, for they may spring from true grief, or they may be a snare. When a woman thinks alone, she thinks evil.

I have found a woman more bitter than death, and a good woman subject to carnal lust. Others again have propounded other reasons why there are more superstitious women found than men. And the first is that they are more credulous; and since the chief aim of the devil is to corrupt faith, therefore he rather attacks them. . . . Women are naturally more impressionable, and more ready to receive the influence of a disembodied spirit; and that when they use this quality well they are very good, but when they use it ill they are very evil.

. . . they have slippery tongues, and are unable to conceal from their fellow-women those things which by evil arts they know; and since they are weak, they find an easy and secret manner of vindicating themselves by witchcraft . . . for it is true that in the Old Testament the Scriptures have much that is evil to say about women and this because of the first temptress, Eve, and her imitators.

The Inquisitors charged that "women are intellectually like children." They are described in Proverbs "as a jewel of gold in a swine's snout." Quoting Valerius to Rufinus, the authors of the *Malleus* thought the following both charming and relevant:

You do know that woman is the Chimera, but it is good that you should know it; for the monster was of three forms; its face was that of a radiant and noble lion, it had the filthy belly of a goat, and it was armed with the virulent tail of a viper. And he means that a woman is beautiful to look upon, contaminating to the touch, and deadly to keep.

The Inquisitors, our early prosecuting attorneys, argued like college professors: "And all this is indicated by the etymology of the word; for *Femina* comes from *Fe* and *Minus*, since she is ever weaker to hold and preserve the faith. . . . Therefore a wicked woman is by her nature quicker to waiver in her faith and consequently quicker to abjure the faith, which is the root of witchcraft."

The stench of the burning bodies of women and the sound of their sizzling flesh must still exude from our genes. Centuries of such unrelenting terror has permitted the male of the species to continue to send the sons of women to war to be senselessly slaughtered and their daughters to be given into countless centuries of cruel and unrelenting servitude to the male of her own species.

After man's separation, he saw the forest, once his home, as wilderness and frightening. But late in the nineteenth century Chief Luther Standing Bear of the Oglala band of Sioux said, "We did not think of the great open plains, the beautiful rolling hills, and the winding streams with tangled growth as 'wild.' Only to the white man was nature a 'wilderness' and only to him was the land 'infested' with 'wild' animals and 'savage' people. To us it was tame. Earth was bountiful and we were surrounded with the blessings of the Great Mystery. Not until the hairy man from the east came and with brutal frenzy heaped injustices upon us and the families we loved was it 'wild' for us. When the very animals of the forest began fleeing from his approach, then it was that for us the 'Wild West' began."

To the Indians, the "Great Mystery" was their father, and the earth their mother. As a child of the earth, the Indian remained in the garden, preserving his relationship with his earth mother and hence his immortality. When the white man came, he did to the Indian what the white man did to himself. He drove the Indian from paradise under the dynamic most often observed in those who are evil or insane: "If I cannot have it, neither can you."

Women, not men, as the givers of life, as nurturers, as, indeed, the mothers of us all, are in sync with the source of life, and power. In the end women and the Great Mother are inseparable. In truth Eve never left the garden. Having never rejected nature or renounced her earth mother, woman is free to return to the garden, with or without her male counterpart, and where woman goes man will shortly follow.

As their last, perhaps only act of decency, men, not God, cast themselves out of the garden. But they have attempted to drag women with them. Yet danger lurks. As women engage men in their battle for power, they join men. As they seek to grasp the illusion of power to which men have desperately held, they, too, become desperate. As they fight for equality with men, they often join men in their frantic, lonely pathology. In coveting men's illusion of power, they also covet men's paranoia, their hate, their ignominious greed. As they fight to grab their share of man's illegitimate power, they fight also to separate themselves from the mother earth. At last, they fight for the equal right to leave the garden. When women ask for equal power they must be aware of the old warning that one should be careful what one asks for lest one's wish be granted.

Man's power is false power. True power is not pathological. True power is not the manifestation of psychosis or panic. The squealing pig caught in the gate, although easily heard, does not bespeak power. True power does not manifest itself in response to the nervous chatter of politicians or the foolish threats and proclamations of frightened, vagrant men wandering outside the garden. True power is not the infamous force of the evil, the foolish, and the greedy exerted upon the innocent. True power is not such power, and in such ways, true power is powerless.

It is said that the universal yearning of strong men is to return to the womb. I say that such yearning is to return to the ways of the mother, to return to the garden, for as Black Elk observed, we all return. All true power forms in a great circle. "You have noticed," he said, "that everything an Indian does is in a circle, and that is because the Power of the World always works in circles, and everything tries to be round.

"In the old days when we were a strong and happy people, all our power came to us from the sacred hoop of the nation and so long as the hoop was unbroken the people flourished. The flowering tree was the living center of the hoop, and the circle of the four quarters nourished it. The east gave peace and light, the south gave warmth, the west gave rain, and the north with its cold and mighty wind gave strength and endurance. This knowledge came to us from the outer world with our religion. Everything the Power of the World does is done in a circle. The Sky is round and I have heard that the earth is round like a ball and so are all the stars. The Wind, in its greatest power, whirls. Birds make their nest in circles, for theirs is the same religion as ours. The sun comes forth and goes down again in a circle. The moon does the same, and both are round.

"Even the seasons form a great circle in their changing, and always come back again to where they were. The life of a man is a circle from childhood to childhood and so it is in everything where power moves. Our tipis were round like the nests of birds and these were always set in a circle, the nation's hoop, a nest of many nests where the Great Spirit meant for us to hatch our children."

It is time for Eve to lead us back to the garden, to complete the great circle of which Black Elk spoke. Men are too sold out, too attached to illegitimate power, too decadent, too afraid, to find their way back. Our brains are like old vines growing up against the burning house. Our souls are like the concrete in which the tiny footprint of the child is embedded. The child has gone.

The child, now grown old, has learned little. In his ignoble search for power man has lost the wisdom of innocence. Were he to stumble on to the garden, he could only stand at a distance and steal furtive glances through the gate. His screaming and scheming, his hollow tactics, his transparent manipulations, his proclamations and protestations, indeed his power, are but the skinny impotence of the child, the lost and lonely child, the wailing child begging to return to his mother. He has completed the circle so that at last, only the mother can hear the child.

# REDESIGNING THE HUMAN MIND

## *The*

## *Tyranny*

## *of the*

## *Media*

*In America freedom is business. If freedom is good for business* we have much freedom. If it is perceived to be bad for business, freedom diminishes accordingly. "60 Minutes" has enjoyed a great following for many years because of the public's perception that it is free to reveal to its viewers that which is not told elsewhere on television. But this is a salable perception, one that has been emulated by others who wish to sell the same commodity. Ratings are what television is about, not freedom, not truth. I dare say if American television could sell lies and falsehoods more profitably, we would never hear another word of truth.

The sale of our names and reputations is also good business. The United States Supreme Court has, through the magic of the law, transformed our good names and reputations into commodities to be sold. If our names are famous they may be sold by the media to a public that craves shock and adores titillation. Under the landmark case, *New York Times v.*

*Sullivan,* publishers can print what they please about public figures, even if what is said or printed is motivated by the publisher's unrelenting enmity and ill will. So long as the publisher claims it did not know of any damaging falsehood the publisher is not liable, and the victim of such defamation bears the burden to prove the contrary.

Libel suits by "public figures" are almost impossible to win, as a consequence of which many of our potential leaders, perhaps our best, stand mute in the political shadows, for should they engage in public debate, they expose themselves to the ubiquitous smearing brush of the media and are rewarded for taking part in democracy by becoming public property that can be sold at every check-out counter in every grocery store in America. Corporate America controls our major networks, magazines, and newspapers. That it should be given unbridled power in the selection of our leaders is a consequence of free speech that carries with it a foreboding potential.

Even a little-known Wyoming cheerleader like Kim Pring, later crowned Miss Wyoming, is not protected under the law. In 1979, *Penthouse* magazine published an obscene story concerning Miss Wyoming in which she was portrayed as such an expert at fellatio she could make men levitate. It was supposedly funny—but it wasn't funny to Kim, who, as a result of the story, was mocked and jeered and finally had to drop out of school. Then she couldn't find a job.

At last, seeking anonymity, she joined the army. I brought the case against *Penthouse,* and a Wyoming jury awarded her $25 million—a fine assessed by the jurors amounting to a dollar for each of *Penthouse*'s claimed 25 million readers. The jury had hoped to stop the sale of innocent people's names and lives for profit. But the United States Court of Appeals reversed the jury's verdict, holding that the writing was protected under the First Amendment. Miss Pring got nothing and *Penthouse* not only kept the profit it gleaned from merchandising its outrageous story, but was freed, indeed encouraged, to do the same in the future.

Things got worse. In 1985 Andrea Dworkin, a life-long and avid fighter against pornography, was attacked by *Hustler*. Her personhood was merchandised in an article containing adjectives that would cause a stout hog to retch. I sued for her as well. But the court held that this was only *Hustler*'s opinion and that the magazine was entitled to express its opinion. Further, the court denied Ms. Dworkin a jury trial even though the Wyoming Constitution guaranteed a jury in all defamation cases. Under the reasoning of the court we can be called rapists, or murderers, or child molesters if the words can be characterized as opinion, and juries are powerless to render justice.[1] The court failed to recognize that *Hustler*'s business is to shock and entertain its readership. It was *Hustler*'s profit, not its freedom, that was protected, for freedom is not freedom when its exercise results in the wanton destruction of the rights of others.

Freedom of the press is the hub upon which the wheel of democracy turns. I argue for robust public debate on every conceivable public issue. I merely argue against an irresponsible media. I argue against giving the media the power to appropriate our good names and those of our potential leaders, of our contributing citizens, of our public persons, and to package them as smut. In short, I argue against the irresponsible attacks on our potential leaders that divert our attention from the issues and that tend to convert public persons to property.

Justice, although often illusive, seems easy enough to understand—that when the media makes a statement about anyone, public figure or private, it should tell the truth, and that if it has negligently or willfully injured that person it should pay for the injury. The

[1] *At this writing the case is pending on Ms. Dworkin's Petition for Reconsideration.*

demand is for simple responsibility. Such was the law of the land for nearly two hundred years until the courts, embracing the commercial requirements of the corporate sector, eliminated the people's right to be free from the wanton desecration of their names, and, instead, protected the media in its sale of our names. Freedom of speech is not freedom to defame, to lie, to injure, or to destroy innocent people. We were guaranteed freedom of speech in order to debate critical issues in the course of self-government. That splendid vision has been sullied by the media itself, which was entrusted with both the exercise and protection of that vital right.

Those who argue most fervently for unlimited rights under the First Amendment are writers and journalists themselves. But in practice these rights do not belong to them, but to their corporate employers. The writer does not enjoy freedom of the press. If his submission violates the editorial policy of the magazine, that is, if the writer's vision of the truth or his belief system is not in sync with that of the magazine, the work will be rejected. If the writer's work could drive away heavy corporate advertisers, the writing, no matter how true, how artful, how vital, may never get ink. Although no brown-shirted censor with his black marker is at work, no one seriously argues that censorship does not exist in this country. But the question is not often addressed: Who censors the media? In America, censorship is vested in those who own the presses. In the end, money censors the media.

Censorship, of course, takes two forms: information withheld and information that is given but fails to reveal the whole truth. The former is called editing, the latter, advertising, in its most blatant form, propaganda. Through carefully created Madison Avenue commercials and with the assistance of behavioral scientists, a corporation will seduce us to buy its product. But the network is not likely to disclose in conjunction with that commercial the numerous charges brought against the corporation for its product's safety. Few corporate advertisers will take part in their own bloodletting. It is no surprise, then, that the media, dependent on its advertisers, directs our attention to human crimes rather than the wrongdoing of its advertisers, although the consequences of corporate crimes may cause those of the individual to look like teddy bears in a grizzlie's den. Daily we gasp at the blood and gore of another murder, but rarely are we shown close-ups of the hundreds of thousands who, on the same day, are suffering their last indescribable agony of cigarette-induced lung cancer. Yet on television the same corporation that merchandises cigarettes to our young sells its food products to us and is held up as one of the nation's good citizens. Daily we are told of another rape, another robbery, but we are not likely to visit the thousands of hospital rooms across the country where, as the result of pollution by a nationally known and respected chemical company, the innocent are dying as their impoverished families look on helplessly.

The selection of news, its focus, its emphasis, its clarity, all deal with a more insidious censorship, one more difficult to detect, one hidden behind scanty details and unimpassioned words that flash quickly by. We are provided the eight-second sound bite that reports the fact of a corporation's theft of millions—but often the fact is presented with the same emphasis as the passing of Groundhog Day. Shortly, on the same network, we will likely see an institutional ad by the offending corporation presenting itself as a wonderfully caring, contributing citizen. The cost of this campaign may run into millions. The ad will perhaps show its workers, decent open faces, speaking in innocent ways about the pride they feel in working for such a company. We will like the workers and forget the corporate crimes that paid for the ad. The corporation will also place ads in newspapers and magazines, showing the corporation as a model of goodwill and decency. Ultimately, such subtle methods by which public opinion is manipulated are often a more insidious censorship than the black marking pencil, for when there is overt censorship the public knows.

In the end, the media prints and broadcasts in accordance with its business requirements. I remember when a certain television network decided that a proposed series starring a well-known country lawyer, who would tell people the truth about the failure of our justice system, would be a hit. The topics were compelling and important to people. They revealed deep-rooted corporate crime. They exposed the helplessness of people who get caught up in the justice system. The series would unveil the myths of freedom that render so many Americans helpless, and the producers believed the series would be an immediate success. Accordingly the network invested hundreds of thousands of dollars in developing this program. The network executives were men of great experience and know-how in reading the public's prevailing appetite. They took part in every aspect of the production. They helped select the stories. They chose the locations. They even edited the dialogue.

But when the network executives presented the pilot they had produced to those who owned and controlled major portions of the network, the series was immediately rejected. No credible explanation was offered. The money used to develop the series was, of course, wasted. When the country lawyer searched his memory for some justifiable reason why the program had failed, he remembered that he had once written uncomplimentary truths about the corporation that now owned a substantial portion of the network—that the corporation owned several insurance companies, that it had been involved in a price-fixing conspiracy and had been required to pay a fine that amounted to only .001% of its net worth, that it had pled guilty in seven cases of price-fixing and had pled *nolo contendere* in thirteen others. The writing told of how the corporation's misfeasance and fraud was said to be so pervasive that the Department of Defense barred the corporation from doing further business with the department—but that 'the suspension lasted for only a month, and that one of its subsidiaries on Wall Street had been implicated in yet another scandal. The country lawyer, of course, was me.

One could hardly blame the corporate owner of the network for refusing to sponsor those who attack and expose it. If we exchanged places I doubt I would have done differently. Indeed, it exceeds all reasonable expectation that the owners of networks should cut their own throats in order to preserve our freedoms. The media has rights as well—to make whatever business decisions it wishes, to forward and protect its interests, to make profits. But those rights are often antithetical to our freedom. As someone once said, "Freedom of the press exists for all who own one."

It is, indeed, a quite incredible, yet uniformly accepted phenomenon, one akin to hiring the wolf to guard the farmer's flock of sheep, that the media, owned by our corporate masters, is the sole voice charged with guarding our individual freedom. But in a society dominated by corporations, the people's power to speak freely and effectively and be heard is the last freedom corporations wish to deliver to the people. The history of corporate resistance to freedom of speech began with the Church itself, the first successful international corporation known to the world, and still today the world's largest. Pope Leo XIII said it plainly: "The liberty of thinking and of publishing whatever one likes . . . that is the fountainhead of many evils."

The danger in America is that people, tied to their televisions for the major portions of their lives, finally come to believe that corporate America speaks for them, that the voice of the New King is, indeed, their voice. If goslings listen to the whining of the fox long enough, they come to believe that the fox is their mother. But in America, the media is the croaking voice of the corporate hawker selling us things. In America, the voice we hear as the voice of freedom is one that continually redesigns our minds to covet the things corporate America seeks to merchandise.

Jerry Mander's classic, *Four Arguments for the Elimination of Television*, tells us that American corporations spend more each year on advertising of their products than the whole country spends on higher education. Seemingly it is more important for us to know which is better for a headache, Anacin or aspirin, than to educate our young. Mander claimed that 83 percent of all network television advertising was attributed to only 100 corporations out of the 400,000 that exist in the country, so that what we see on television chiefly suits the mentality and purposes of those hundred corporations. Mander says, " . . . without currying their favor the networks would cease to exist. . . . It is no accident that television has been dominated by a handful of corporate powers. Neither is it accidental that television has been used to re-create human beings into a new form that matches the artificial, commercial environment."

To put the matter in perspective, there are no Indians, no blacks, no women, no working people, no Buddhists, no revolutionaries, no artists, no socialists, to name a few, who are major advertisers on television. The National Organization for Women does not have money to sponsor "Roseanne," were it so inclined. Labor unions do not sponsor "Monday Night Football." Teachers' organizations cannot sponsor a science program. And even public television is dependent on corporate advertisers. Corporate America determines what electronic primary experiences our children shall have, where, on any given evening, we shall travel and what we shall see, and from what perspective. It decides what news we will hear, what blood on what streets, what deaths, what crime, what scandals. It is frightening to realize that corporations with mind-altering electronics possess the power to control 250 million mostly unsuspecting subjects. As a consequence we have been converted from lovers of freedom to lovers of things sold by the corporate sponsor: We are not sensitive to changes in the status of our freedom but to changes in the formula of Coke Classic. Most of us do not march in the streets, we march, instead, down to McDonald's because we "deserve a break today."

The immensely rich and powerful corporations of this country can buy access to the public mind, can form public taste, and can create public opinion. These corporations can invade our minds and change our likes or dislikes, our ideas, our values, and even our personalities. The citizen has no such power. Since we, the people, are a conglomerate of our collective experiences, and since the average household has its television set going six hours a day, it is no exaggeration to assert that in America we are creatures born not of our blood mothers but of our corporate mothers, who have spawned us through television.

Mander states that the best environment for advertising is a dull and even one, one in which we hear canned laughter, in which no thought is required, in which nothing competes with the excitement of the advertisement. I was talking to a photographer friend the other day while he carefully set up the artificial lighting to take my photograph. I wondered why the photographer didn't take advantage of the natural light. We were outdoors. The sun made wonderful lattices through the quaking aspens. Their shadows were like the receding lines of picket fences. Why not allow me to simply be part of this wonderful, natural light and reveal me as I am, a man attached to trees and to sun and to shadows?

"Photojournalism is nearly a thing of the past," he said.

"Why?" I asked. "I should think that it would be poised for bigger and better things."

"No," he said. "Advertisers want calm, serene photographs in the magazines. They want a passive mood.

A visual that is dynamic, startling, exciting, or passionate, competes with their ads. They want nothing more visually stimulating in the magazine than their advertisement." He looked sad and then turned his reflectors to eliminate the shadows of the aspens.

Freedom of speech is another of those notions that exists in myth but not in practice. John Quincy Adams once said of freedom of speech, "No such thing ever existed. No such thing now exists," and of course he was right. We exhibit great tolerance for those who share our views, but for those who do not, we extend little freedom. Minorities who speak out are uniformly prosecuted in one form or another. Those who hold views differing from our own are often destroyed. The "witch hunts" of the McCarthy days immediately come to mind. We remember those who fought and demonstrated against the Vietnam War. Today those who speak out on either side of the abortion issue are targeted. Those who speak either for or against gays become victims. Those who hate Jews or blacks as well as those who fight for their rights pay the penalty. Environmentalists, labor organizers, whistle-blowers, euthanasiasts, animal lovers, nudists, communists, nonconformists, those who support or fight pornography, those who support or oppose uncensored art, all are eventually punished for expressing their views. They may be punished by exclusion or banishment. Some will lose their jobs. Some will lose financial support. Some will be silenced by prosecutions. Some will be infiltrated by government agents and snitches. Some will be set up and entrapped. Some will be libeled. Some will be locked in penitentiaries. Some will be shot. But all will be hurt, physically, emotionally, or financially, for saying what they believe.

Few social psychologists doubt that redesigning the human mind has become the long-term objective of corporate America. That objective has, in major part, been accomplished. We have adopted the religion of free enterprise that permits the rich and the powerful to starve the poor and the powerless merely as a function of "keeping score." We have delivered the voice of freedom, our voice, to the New King, the corporate oligarchy. Our instincts of independence have been replaced with feelings of impotence. We have become more domesticated and docile than independent and free. We have delivered our power to our oppressors in exchange for their promise that we will be safe. At last, we have accepted the myths of freedom as fact in the place of freedom itself.

We love our servitude. But why not? It often feels as good as freedom, and we can enjoy it without the risk that always accompanies the struggle for freedom. We can wave our flags on the Fourth of July and look at our neighbors who are more enslaved than we, and that reassures us. We can say truthfully that we enjoy more freedom than any nation in the world. In America we can love freedom, love it to death. We can wrap ourselves in the flag and, so long as we do not have to suffer for it, so long as we keep faith with the New King, so long as we believe we have it, or its reasonable facsimile, we are as good as free, are we not?

As I write these lines I feel the pangs of fear that grip the hearts of all who love liberty and know of its fragile nature. In the title of this book I have suggested that we have come "from freedom to slavery." That, of course, is not entirely accurate. Many Americans have never been free. Many have been born into slavery, a slavery of poverty, a slavery of myth, a slavery of false gods, a slavery to ideas that are no longer true or that have never been true. As the saying goes, the more things change the more they stay the same. There was a time when a black slave could purchase his freedom from his master. Today those who enjoy the greatest freedom are those who have the wherewithal to buy it. At last, even freedom, has become a commodity, indeed, an item of luxury.

To be sure, we have made great advancements. Americans no longer sit in the back of buses because of their color. We have elected a black woman to the United States Senate. Black mayors hold office in our major cities. We have black coaches in the NFL and elsewhere. Women enjoy power they have never before experienced. Gays have come out of their closets. As a nation we are more sensitive to our mother earth. Yet these advancements also permit us to lull in our apathy. Focused on these accomplishments we are likely to see them as evidence of our freedom when, indeed, they are merely scraps to distract the baying hounds. The corporate oligarchy understands that its power is safe only so long as the people *believe* they are free, and corporate America has the means—the exclusive means—by which to create and sell that fantasy. The recurring theme in these writings has been that we have been served an illusion of freedom like so many vaporous potatoes on a plate that magically disappear into the mist whenever we try to stick our fork in them. In the end, the most deadly trap of all is a brainwashed mind, for the brain, washed against itself, is powerless.

Perhaps the most blatant betrayal of our freedom came during this century when the Federal Communications Commission, charged with regulating the use of our airways, instead delivered them to corporate America. What I am saying is simple and frightening: An agency of the United States government, the FCC, effectively transformed our airways into commodities and handed them over to the corporate entities that exploit us. Left with no means by which to engage in communication with each other, we became estranged, ineffective, and at last impotent. We became a people without thoughts of our own, without ideas, without values or viewpoints of our own to be shared with each other in the fullfillment of the democratic dream. Instead, we, ourselves, became commodities to be sold in the media's marketplace.

I say we, too, were marketed. When we sit down to watch what purports to be the evening news we are being sold. We are an audience with a high value. Every program, from football to MTV, gathers its specific audience in the same way that the fisherman nets perch or halibut or salmon, depending on the market's demand. As fish in the net, we are sold to the advertisers as so many hundreds of thousands of middle-aged persons, or kids, or teenagers, or the affluent. We no longer speak back. We no longer speak to each other. We no longer speak at all. We are only silent. Silent listeners. And as water washes the rocks smooth and at last wears them away, so, too, our brains are washed into intellectual oblivion. With an evil magic, the brainwashing transforms our children from the bright, the inquiring and the creative to mindless consumers, to empty-headed shoppers concerned chiefly with things, and the means by which to acquire things. The brainwashing turns our children into things for sale, things in the pursuit of things, things chasing dollars and the things dollars will purchase. The brainwashing has dehumanized us. It has left us comporting ourselves like lumpen slobs drooling at the trough where we are slopped like anthropomorphic hogs with the vacuous fare corporate America throws at us.

The FCC could have, indeed, had the duty to make the airways available to a wide variety of interests that represent a free citizenry. The airways should have been assigned to television stations controlled by labor, by blacks, by women, by environmentalists, by small businesspeople, by educators, by farmers, by workers, in short, by the American people. Instead, without consideration—free—the FCC gave our airways to three mammoth corporations who now own them as their private property and, with other networks that have since come into existence, perfect the redesigning of our minds into those of the perfect consumer. Our minds have also been reformed to adopt a single virulent philosophy, a supposed wisdom—that to prosper, Americans must support the dribble-down theory of the New King, that to survive, Americans must abdicate their power to the corporate conglomerate.

The FCC, itself a hopelessly entangled bureaucracy, one ultimately controlled by the gargantuan corporations it seeks to regulate, has repeatedly proven it cannot exercise its power to preserve our rights. In fact, it no longer harbors any intent to do so. The corporations who own the networks are too large, too powerful, too entwined into the power structure to be controlled. ABC was swallowed up by Capital Cities Communications. NBC was scooped up by General Electric when it purchased NBC's parent, RCA. The FCC, itself, has become a part of the intimate corporate family. Its members and functionaries pass back and forth through the revolving door, today purportedly regulating the corporation, tomorrow, as their reward for good and faithful service, occupying a posh position in the very corporations they regulated yesterday.

Justice Brandeis in *Whitney v. California* said, "Those who won our independence believed . . . that public discussion is a political duty," as, indeed, it is. Justice Brennan in *New York Times v. Sullivan* said, "thus we consider this case against the background of a profound national commitment to the principle that debate on public issues should be uninhibited, robust, and wide-open. . . . " But how can we perform our public duty unless we control the means by which to communicate with each other? Worse, how can we be free when we are constantly reeling under the sedative of corporate propaganda? In retrospect, how could self government have been so easily destroyed by the simple devise of delivering our airways to the New King?

The First Amendment guarantees our free speech. By implication it also guarantees the people's right to own and control the means by which the people can speak to each other. One would not claim the ownership of a useful interest in a car unless one also owned the wheels. Further, the fact that our airways have been stolen from us these many years does not eliminate our ownership of them. Time does not create a cure for an original wrong. If we steal our neighbor's cow, we cannot argue that although we stole her, we nevertheless fed her for fifteen years, and, therefore, she now belongs to us.

Equally lamentable is the fact that that which has been stolen from us has been thereafter served back to us in the lowest form yet imaginable. It is as if our wheat has been stolen and we have been left to choke in the chaff. In their defense, advertisers and network executives contend that the American public is an unintelligent, unthinking, rustic conglomerate of dolts. "Look," they argue, "at what the people choose to watch." As one executive told me, "The viewers, themselves, demand the garbage we feed them. If they demanded a different cuisine we would feed that to them, as well." Another put it more succinctly: "We, in television, rise to the highest level of our audience. The highest level of our audience, unfortunately, is at the age of an average thirteen-year-old."

I do not dismiss so easily the intelligence, the taste, or the wisdom of the American people. It is not the level of the people's intelligence that limits us, but the constant barrage of insipid, tasteless rubbish that is relentlessly dumped on us as if we live in the bottom of an intellectual land fill. And how could it be otherwise for advertisers? Most of the products hawked on television are utterly irrelevant to the good life we seek. Madison Avenue knows, of course, that, in an intelligent environment, it cannot sell that which is patently worthless. One is not as likely to buy sugar corn pops as a result of watching a conference considering the health hazards of America's diet as one is likely to buy the same cereal as a result of watching some empty-headed sit-com.

I have tried too many cases before ordinary people sitting as jurors without developing a profound respect for their inherent, collective wisdom, their ability to absorb complicated facts, and their capacity to thereafter come up with a just result. It is easy to put the

American public down. But those who believe that intelligence and taste, indeed, wisdom, are traits reserved only for corporate moguls and Wall Street bankers are the fools. People know. The collective intelligence of the American citizenry is awesome if, after it is fully informed, it is given a chance to honestly express itself. On the other hand, there is little doubt that if our intellectual diet consists of that which is currently offered on television, the old saying has relevance: "Garbage in—garbage out."

Television producers argue that people want to be entertained. Of course. But that does not mean that people do not also want to be enlightened, delighted, and uplifted, and it does not mean that people do not want to be informed. Despite the myths of freedom that fog our clear vision, in the basement of their minds the people know they are trapped. They know they are rarely told the whole truth. They know their vote ultimately makes little difference. They know that they usually do not and cannot get justice. If one knows that one's fervent striving makes little difference and that the whole truth is a rarity, if one knows one is the object of continuous exploitation from every quarter and is helpless to do much about it, then entertainment is the answer, as escape and denial also become the answers.

I do not disrespect the intelligence of the people. I disrespect those who have, by their own deep scorn and arrogance, so demeaned the people for so long that the prophesy of the people's intellectual impotence has often been fulfilled. But when we have taken back our power, when we again control our airways and our voices can again be heard on every major issue that effects our freedom, when we know that we truly guide the ship of state, the character of the media will have also changed. Then truth, then in-depth analysis, then the presentation of facts (no matter how complex), then responsibility, yes, then art, too, will take precedent over the silly, the mundane, the false and the empty. Then, with the repossession of our airways, the people will begin a new adventure—the quest for the long-awaited American dream.

# KINGDOM OF THE SELF

*The*

*Tyranny*

*of*

*Time*

*Dear Bob,*[1]

On this snowy Christmas day I look out on the majestic Grand, the top of its peak shrouded in an oncoming storm. No matter how relentless and bitter the cold, how deep the snow, how powerful the winds, the mountain seems never to change—no more than a passing thought or a brief encounter brings change to us. Yet, in imperceptible ways the mountain bears the marks of every storm, and like us, my dear friend, even the mountain is not immortal.

I am told the Grand is a young mountain, that like a sprouting adolescent it grows a couple of inches a year. I see it as a rowdy teenager—uncivilized, unrestrainable, unpredictable. As for the storm, I think the mountain has no patience. When the mountain tires of the tumult and racket, it does not wait

[1] *Robert R. Rose, for many years my law partner, and the former Chief Justice of the Wyoming Supreme Court.*

for the sun. It merely shrugs the storm away. But as inevitably as we grow old, so too will the mountain. I have seen the tops of old peaks worn nearly to the valley floor, the granite creased and wrinkled, the surface as smooth as a baby's cheeks. Yet they are still mountains. They are still fighting storms. At last they are still engaged in the ultimate folly—of simply standing there.

I think of all of the storms you have survived, and the courage I have taken from witnessing how you have weathered them. You have accepted your travails as if they were but vagrant clouds. I have seen the blizzards blind your eyes so that you could not read the words you wrote on the page, and I have witnessed the terrible fury that has descended upon your lungs. And still you are there, and like the mountain, an aura of joy soon enough shines through. That is the great mystery of your being. And of the mountain's.

On this Christmas day, and during this same storm, our young bitch, Rosebud, had her first litter of pups. When the first pup was born she licked it clean, and nudged it to her, and it nourished itself even before its littermates were born. For each, in kind, she did the same. My own dear Imaging crawled into Rosebud's little closet and stayed with her until all the pups were born. It was late and I knew Imaging was tired, and that from her long ordeal with the surgery, her back must have been very painful—especially crouched down with Rosebud in that tight little closet. I tried to convince Imaging to come to bed.

"I need to be here," she said.

"Rosebud knows more about having pups than you and I," I argued. "Dogs have been having pups for millions of years." Imaging didn't answer. "Come on, honey," I said. "She'll be all right."

"I want to be here," she said. Then she sort of half whispered to herself, "You don't understand."

And Imaging was right, of course. I do not understand. I am not wise enough to put this all together. I think you and Imaging know more about this process than I. I think old mountains also know. I think your wisdom, yours and the mountains', keeps you from defiling this knowledge with words.

I had a conversation the other day with the mason who had just finished the fireplace in our home. It was built of huge granite boulders that had been dumped by the countless trainloads at the foot of the mountain about ten thousand years ago when the last glacier receded—"glacial garbage," the geologists call it. Some of the boulders weighed several tons, and the mason brought in a hoist to lift the rock. The finished product was simple but monumental. The mason and I stood together admiring his work. A good pine fire was snapping away.

"Well, John,"[2] I said, "you've achieved a little bit of immortality here."

"How's that?" He looked surprised.

"This fireplace will be here long after we're both gone."

"I suppose you're right," he said.

"And a hundred years from now nobody will remember who owned this house or who built this fireplace. Both our names will probably have been lost to history. But this fireplace will still be heating somebody's back side and bringing pleasure. You should get a lot of satisfaction out of that."

The man didn't say anything. He just gazed into the fire, and the fire lighted his face, and he looked very beautiful.

Our names are important—but mostly to us. Immortality is usually nameless. A strange dynamic is at work here. Immortality is unconscious of itself. Those who seek it seem never to achieve it. Immortality is like trying to grab hold of one's breath on a cold winter's day. One only grabs hold of oneself. I think people

[2]John Bernardis of Casper, Wyoming, an extraordinary man as solid as his rocks and mortar.

**197**

who are unmindful of their contributions make the most lasting gifts—a mother who, by loving her child, teaches her child to love; a teacher who, adoring the innocent passion of the child, confirms for the child that it is all right to sing, and to spread joy; your own great gifts of love to generations of young lawyers who have seen you as a role model, as a lawyer, as a judge, as a man who has made us proud to be lawyers.

Names soon fade on both the headstones in the cemetery and the headstones of human memory. You can walk through any graveyard and see the markers, many toppled over, the names beginning to disappear— "In memory of our beloved father, Jason W——" . . . I could not make out the last letters. I remember picking up a small stone that had once marked the grave of a child. It had been dislodged, by what or whom I could not guess. I turned it over and put it back in its place. Although the name had been worn away, I could still make out one word that had endured the years: DARLING.

I held that small, cold, white stone in my hands. Those who had adored their "darling" were gone. And those who had loved them were likely gone as well. What survives? Love survives. But fear also survives— and superstition. I thought of the endless generations of mothers who believe their innocent babies are somehow born in sin, and that if their babies should die before the priests get their hands upon them, their children's little souls would be condemned to bob endlessly on the dark seas of purgatory. When, please, when was that darling child soaked in the evil brine? Such a notion was the *original* sin, an idea born of men who could not bear the thought that, considering the condition of their own tarnished souls, they, too, had once been innocent babes. I should think it better that men accept the full width and breadth of their transgressions as the price paid for growth and wisdom rather than unloading their sins on every newborn found at its mother's breast.

Yet love, indeed, survives best. You, my friend, have already proven that. One young lawyer who has learned from your model that it is all right for lawyers to care about their clients and to fight for them can, in a short lifetime, touch many, and they, in turn, multitudes. Caring is contagious. In the end, love and joy and fear and hate are all immortal. With every breath, with every word, with every act, we touch eternity.

As for wisdom, well, it, too, is like the fog. It can be seen. Yet we can walk right through it. And when we think we have it, it vanishes. I have read thousands of those brittle opinions by the judges of our highest courts, and I have learned nothing. Nothing at all! I have learned more from my children and my dogs than I ever learned from the scholars' dry and scaly volumes. This much I know: Truth, whatever it is, is simple. Truth, if we shall ever find it, can be understood by even the most humble.

And, my friend, I have learned more from my clients than from all the experts and great men of science I have encountered. We can never forget the horribly injured we have fought for in the courtrooms—a father with critical parts of his brain destroyed, a woman carried into court on a litter who could not speak a word or even sit up, a paralyzed child, a mother with no arms to hold her baby, the terrorized poor, charged by the state with crimes they did not commit? They seemed so helpless! Yet they became the most powerful persons in the courtroom. Our clients have taught us that we have all the power we need—all the power to live, all

the power to bloom and to seed, all the power to endure, yes, and, at last, all the power we need to die.

Religions! Ah, what religions do to us! How they
supplant thought! How they fence out reason! How
they render us impotent! How they poison us. The idea
that one country, one people, one system is the chosen
system—those ideas are religions. Capitalism and communism are both religions that once left us standing
helplessly by while the world's leaders, in the name of
their respective religions, plotted to destroy the world.
The idea that the poor are poor because they are lazy,
and that the rich are rich because they are not, is part
of the dogma of free enterprise and leaves half the
world famished and in rags. "Progress" has become an
icon in the Church of Money and Things. Youth and
Beauty are the new gods of television. The idea that
people are valuable only if they can convert themselves
into salable commodities, that the earth was created for
the exploitation of man, that men stand above women,
that some certain race excels, that the human species
is superior to the other inhabitants of the planet—all
such ideas exist as religions. Religions—whether spiritual, secular, political, scientific, economic, or social—
all demand faithful acceptance. Religions are cages of
the mind.

I have seen many of our best and brightest captured at birth by religions, their minds bound like the
feet of little Chinese girls which in years past had also
been religiously bound. When the babies became
women their feet remained stunted. I remember seeing many of these old women in China still hobbling
about on their piteously crippled stumps. In the same
way, I am saddened when I see whole populations, presumably without values of their own, become bound
up by the ideas of tyrants, of reformers, of dema-
gogues, of power mongers, and hawkers of the beads
and trinkets of our culture.

I am saddened when I see people who, born free,
deliver their freedom to government, and then be-

seech their politicians not to sell them out to the highest bidder, to their enemies, to the corporate power center that will further enslave them. I am saddened to see valuable people selling their lives to soulless entities who consume them like any expendable material, like fuel, like fodder, like rags and parts are consumed. That people have accepted themselves as mere things to be bought and sold is part of a pernicious religion.

How often you have heard me beg young lawyers not to sell themselves to the giant law firms of the country where, like common harlots, they will be chosen from the line to labor by the hour at the pleasure of whichever corporate client chooses to engage them. Remember the corporate discards who have come to us after having devoted their lives to their corporate employers only to discover that although loyalty has been earned, it is never repaid? The cruel irony persists— Those who, on behalf of their corporate masters, have been most ardent in sucking out the last drop of blood from the poor and the powerless are, themselves, on a conveyer belt to the same slaughterhouse, and when at last they reach the man with the hammer, they discover there is no way off the belt. You remember how they have come to us, the executives as often as the lowest lackeys—and in the end there was true democracy there, for they were all treated the same? You remember their bitter disappointments, their sense of having been used up and wasted, their feelings of betrayal, and how, too late, they learned that the corporation was not made up of people, but that, instead, the corporation was a consumer of people?

On the other hand, the cry, "Power to the people!" has become a disconcerting irrelevancy. We, the people, already have the power. We, the people, have always had the power. We need no leaders to achieve it, no religions to claim it, no politics to express it. Our power does not come from parents or spouses or employers or the block captain or the priest or from God.

If I understand that simple proposition I have changed, the change is mammoth. The change is explosive. *The change is freedom.*

I remember when I began to feel my own power. Somehow I had discovered the King within—the King of the self. I was fearful of the King, in awe of him. Yet in his presence I felt no servitude to man, to government, to law or to God. I felt as if I could conquer any obstacle, win any case. Sometimes my enthusiasm amused you. Sometimes you tested these new powers. But always you gave me room. And you were patient. Sometimes I think you mistook my enthusiasm for courage. Perhaps at times you even admired it. I now know what I did not know then: My exuberance merely paid homage to my newly discovered *kingdom of the self.* I shudder to think what might occur if all of the earth's people awakened their own inner Kings. This much I can predict: Magically, overnight, the world would be free.

When we acknowledge the *kingdom of the self,* we will no longer accept slavery either for ourselves or for others, no matter how it is disguised, for the King cannot tolerate slavery. When we acknowledge the *kingdom of the self,* we will no longer tolerate untruths, for the King cannot tolerate manipulations and lies. When we acknowledge the *kingdom of the self,* we will no longer permit the children of the world to be tarred with fear and feathered with guilt, for the King cannot tolerate such abuse of the world's children. And when we stop abusing our children we will finally enjoy peace.

Yet the problem is that most reformers want our power. Our political reformers offer political reform in exchange for our power. Our social reformers offer social reform in exchange for our power. Jesus wanted God to have our power. His priests want the power for the Church. The price we usually pay for reform is the delivery of our power to the reformers, whoever they may be.

You, my friend, know I honor the law so long as the law honors the people. You know I am arguing neither for anarchy nor against a representative form of government. In the larger sense of government we must be represented. But representation is not abdication. It is different from surrender. The King always acts through his representatives. But the King does not deliver his power to his representatives. We, as King of ourselves, must always reserve to ourselves our own power. That idea is ingrained in our system, but the idea has somehow been forgotten. Madison understood that the American system was "altogether different" from the British because "the people, not the government, possess the absolute sovereignty." Or, as Madison had said earlier in the House, "the censorial power is in the people over the Government, and not the Government over the people." We should dispatch mere delivery persons to Congress, those who will carry our votes as we cast them, rather than sending those who, possessing our power, deliver our votes to the corporate core in exchange for power.

Your decisions from the high court in Wyoming were uncommon decisions based on common sense and common justice—a simple acknowledgment of what is right and what is wrong for the human species. Strange that justice requires no machination of thought, no frilly rhetoric, no intricate syntax. Your decisions were not radical. But justice is usually labeled as radical while injustice is often accepted as the standard. Yet we remember that once slavery in America was not seen as radical. It became, instead, a revolutionary idea that slaves should be freed. When we have lived under a pernicious power long enough, no matter how oppressive, we grow so accustomed to the yoke that its removal seems frightening, even wrong.

For more than two hundred years, like evil termites, disenfranchising ideas have gnawed away at the supporting timbers of American democracy. From the beginning, women have been vassalized. So have minorities. So have workers and artists and lovers of the earth. Far more deracinating is the historic progression in America that finds living people governed by nonliving corporations, that in a democracy nonliving corporations should own our legislatures, buy our presidents, select our judges, possess our airways, pollute our rivers, foul our oceans, and poison our skies.

It is a wholly radical idea that people should be encouraged to horde wealth without restraint, to nurture their avarice to full madness without caring for their less-fortunate neighbors who have been exploited in the process. It is a radical idea that we should destroy the earth, our home, and that we should ardently demand an unlimited right to continue in this demented act of terracide. The most radical of all ideas is that profit is more important than human dignity, more sacred than human life. Over the years those in power have endowed these radical, often cruel and illogical rules with the dignity of right and law. That which is patently unjust has become justice. That which is obviously wrong has become right. That which opposes the position of power has always been labeled as radical.

Our minds are like the willows along a high mountain stream that have been bent and bowed by the heavy winter snows. In the spring, the snows are melted away. And although the willows bounce back, one can easily tell the direction in which the snows have bent them. It takes a good deal of bending of willows in the opposite direction to ever get them righted. One bending is not enough.

It is now obvious to me that if there is worth in our lives, it is not because we have discovered anything new, but because we, as many before us, have rediscovered for ourselves simple truths. We are but a part of the process, of man's eternal attempt to right the willows of the mind. What we have seen and what we have said to each other will be repeated again and again, until the species shall have risen above myth, above religion, above the dull and mindless acceptance of ideas that bring hurt and enslavement to the human race, until the willows of the mind shall have been righted against the snows of tyranny. Then, at last, we shall be free.

*When I came down this morning to see what the night had* wrought, there in Rosebud's little closet lay seven tiny Labrador puppies, as black as little black rats, their eyes tightly closed so as not to view the harsh world too soon. And there lay Rosebud weary from the rigors of the night, her puppies already sucking. Imaging, too, still lay sleeping, exhausted from having partaken in this magical affair called "life."

The snow continues to cover the valley. Now the Grand is completely hidden, and you, my friend, seem far away. Yet I am connected to you, connected by life and on some dark day, by death, and by the eternal process that is God. I am also connected to the mountain and to Rosebud and to her puppies. I still cannot put this all together. I still do not understand. But I know that Rosebud and her pups, and Imaging, and you and the mountain, are all involved in this conspiracy of life, and death—that it is the process that must be cherished. I now see, my dear friend, that I, too, am part of this, that it is impossible for me to know more, and if I did, I would no longer be free.

*Love,*

Gerry
Christmas Day, 1992

# A C K N O W L E D G M E N T S

*This*

*Guy*

*Weil*


*It was the Fourth of July and this guy Weil had been sitting* in the back of the room where I was holding forth to a bunch of writers in Jackson Hole, Wyoming, on the subject of freedom, which I think is more of an idea in this country than a reality, and when the speech was over he comes up to me and says I should write a book about it.

"Yeah, thank you very much," I said back. "That's a good idea. Everybody's written a book about freedom, so why shouldn't I?" He could tell I was joking him.

"They haven't written *your* book," Weil said. And he let it go at that.

A couple of days later I get a letter from this same guy, who I find out is a senior editor at St. Martin's Press. The letter was written along the margins of a page out of the *New York Times*. The page was a reproduction of the Declaration of Independence that the *Times* had published to celebrate the Fourth of July. He wrote: *Perhaps your words, your thoughts, your all-too-palpable anger, your explosive indignation about inequality, slavery and rampant materialism, all need to be expressed in another form.*

This guy is different from the ones I've encountered in the business. He's alive, and smart, and creative—actually creative—and in a business that's about creativity, it's rare to find anybody who's had a fresh idea since the urge was stomped out of them in kindergarten. In this business people treat fresh ideas like something that hurts their sinuses.

After forty years in the law my life has become a reaction against the breathing dead. But this guy had enthusiasm, and he rode his ideas like a buckeroo on a wild horse. I thought, There's hope for the publishing industry yet. I swear I couldn't help it. I wrote the book for him. But if you don't like it, which I think is unlikely, you should petition this guy, Bob Weil, to get your money back. Remember, the book was his idea, not mine.

*Gerry Spence*

# NOTES BY CHAPTER

*Chapter 4.* "The Invisible Trap." The statistics concerning the destruction of the earth were gleaned from the scholarly and insightful article by David W. Orr. "What Is Education For?" appearing in *Earth Ethics,* spring 1992. The reference to a species as a "pilgrim of four billion years of evolution" is Gary Snyder's in "An End to Birth," published in *Earth Ethics,* fall 1992.

*Chapter 7.* "The New Indians." The historical data concerning the American Revolution, and the Constitution, the quotes from Thomas Paine, from John Adams, the attitudes of Washington and Lord Dunsmore toward slaves in their armies, the Maryland County report as well as the quote of Alexander Hamilton, are all from that brave and bright work of truth by Howard Zinn, *A People's History of the United States,* Harper and Row, 1980.

My figures on the earth's population now and at the end of the next century together with Donella H. Meadows's quotations, came from *Earth Ethics,* vol. 4, no. 1, "Population, Poverty and Planet Earth," by Donella H. Meadows.

The Indian quotations are all from that beautiful collection by T. C. McLuhan, entitled, *Touch the Earth,* Simon and Schuster, 1971.

*Chapter 9.* "Eve's Return to the Garden." Again I have gone to *Touch the Earth,* Simon and Schuster, 1971, for the Indian quotes. The quotations from the *Malleus Maleficarum of Heinrich Kramer and James Sprenger* were translated by the Reverend Montague Summers and published by Dover Publications, Inc., New York, 1971.

*Chapter 10.* "Redesigning the Human Mind." The references to Jerry Mander's classic work, indeed, the title to this chapter, came from *Four Arguments for the Elimination of Television,* Quill, New York, 1978.

# ABOUT THE AUTHOR

*Gerry Spence was born and educated in the small towns of* Wyoming where he has practiced law for over forty years. People ask, How does a small-town lawyer who lives in Jackson Hole, Wyoming, maintain a national law practice? Spence gives the answer: "All you have to do is wear a big Stetson and look tough."

Yet those who know Gerry Spence know differently. He has spent his lifetime representing the poor, the injured, the forgotten, and the damned against what Spence calls "the New King"—mammoth corporations and mammoth government, against power and the indifference of power. He has never lost a criminal case and has received more million-dollar verdicts for injured citizens than any lawyer in America. His power as an orator is awesome but he is at his best when he turns his wrath against the "nonbreathers," as Spence calls Corporate America, the power structure that robs people of their lives, their rights, their freedom and renders us the "new slaves."

This is Spence's fifth book. It has been preceded by *Gunning for Justice, Of Murder and Madness, Trial by Fire,* and *With Justice for None.* The author is also a noted painter, poet, and photographer. The photographs within are his.